This book will bless not only young ⸻ ⸻ ⸺son who wants
the beauty of God to shine brightly
resource for all who want to accur⸺
—**Amy Baker**, ACBC Certified
Picture Perfect

CW01500729

This devotional is both tenderly c ⸺
Read this book and buy one for a friend!
—**Ellen Mary Dykas**, Director of Equipping for Ministry to
Women, Harvest USA; Author

Andrea shares how God's Word has met her in her struggles, bring-
ing hope and transformation. You will discover the beauty, value, and
purpose that God has lovingly given your embodied soul!
—**Liz Edrington**, Author, *Anxiety: Finding the Better Story*

Andrea gently guides the reader to see that her loving Creator God
has designed her well. As a counselor, I will regularly use this book.
—**Kristen Hatton**, Licensed Professional Counselor; Author,
Face Time: Your Identity in a Selfie World

Anyone who has struggled with body image, insecurity, and shame
knows how complex and particular a struggle it is. Andrea Lee tenderly guides readers to the gospel with compassion, nuance, and biblical wisdom. What a gift to be counseled by this devotional!
—**Ashley Kim**, Writer; Student, Columbia University

This devotional invites any teenage girl who struggles with body-
image issues to look upward daily to the loving-kindness of their
God and Savior, who speaks truthfully, gently, and compassionately
into relentless and crushing thoughts, feelings, and experiences con-
cerning their bodies.
—**Monica Kim**, Director of Care and Counseling, Hope Montco
Church, Ambler, Pennsylvania

An exceptional 31-day devotional. God-focused and full of Scripture, hope, and practical biblical tips. I highly recommend it.
—**Martha Peace**, Biblical Counselor; Author

This resource will refuel and encourage those who seek endurance in the race from a broken body to a redeemed, eternal body. Readers will feast on God's Word and leave the table feeling satisfied in Christ.

—**Melissa C. Powell**, Assistant Professor, Department of Health and Human Performance, University of Tennessee at Chattanooga

Andrea engages the sensitive topic of body image with empathy and hope—she understands because she has waged her own personal battles on this front. She entreats readers to consider that God, not our bodies, is the ultimate source of true peace and joy. Her daily reflections will help you set your mind on the delightful treasure that is Jesus Christ, and in so doing, to find peace with the good gift of your body, which God created for a purpose.

—**Hayley Satrom**, Author; Codirector, Heart Song Counseling

Our bodies were designed to help us worship God, encounter the wonders of his creation, and serve others. God wants you to enjoy the unique body he has given you! If body-image struggles are making that enjoyment feel impossible, Andrea Lee can help you experience your body with increasing peace and joy.

—**Jenny Solomon**, Author; Cofounder, Solomon SoulCare

In concise, biblically focused devotional entries, Andrea Lee provides important theological truth in a package that is easy to read and digest but that leaves room for further contemplation and discussion. I can't wait to use this book with my own counselees.

—**Jocelyn Wallace**, Biblical Counselor; Conference Speaker; Author, *Helping Children with Body Shame*

BODY IMAGE

31-DAY DEVOTIONALS
FOR TEENAGERS

A Series

CHELSEA KINGSTON ERICKSON
Series Editor

Anxiety: Finding the Better Story, by Liz Edrington
Body Image: Valuing God's Good Gift, by Andrea Lee
Identity: Discovering Who You Are in Christ, by Lindsey Carlson

BODY IMAGE

Valuing God's Good Gift

ANDREA LEE

P U B L I S H I N G
P.O. BOX 817 • PHILLIPSBURG • NEW JERSEY 08865-0817

Cover design by Jelena Mirkovic

Printed in the United States of America

Library of Congress Cataloging-in-Publication Data

Names: Lee, Andrea, M. A., author.
Title: Body image : valuing God's good gift / Andrea Lee.
Description: Phillipsburg, New Jersey : P&R Publishing Company, [2025] |
    Series: 31-day devotionals for teenagers | Audience: Ages Teenagers |
    Audience: Grades 10-12 | Summary: "In this imperfect world, even good
    gifts-like your body!-come with major challenges. Over 31 days, learn
    how to pursue and enjoy God's good purpose for your embodied life"--
    Provided by publisher.
Identifiers: LCCN 2024051261 | ISBN 9798887790770 (paperback) | ISBN
    9798887790787 (epub)
Subjects: LCSH: Teenage girls--Religious life. | Body image in
    girls--Religious aspects--Christianity. | Body image--Biblical teaching.
    | Devotional calendars.
Classification: LCC BV4551.3 .L44 2025 | DDC 248.8/33--dc23/eng/20250109
LC record available at https://lccn.loc.gov/2024051261

For Darien

Your love and leadership made this book possible.
I'm so grateful for you.

CONTENTS

UNITED TO CHRIST

RESTORED TO GOD

INTRODUCTION

You've probably picked up this book because you have painful thoughts about your body. You might feel like your body doesn't express who you really are. You might be frustrated because your best efforts to make your body fit your ideal aren't working. You may be baffled by why you think about your body all the time and why you feel so much shame about it. You may feel isolated as you wrestle with the challenges of a disability that the people around you don't understand. You may be constantly comparing yourself to others, always coming up short.

Struggles over body image can bring deep anguish and crushing hopelessness. I've known the pain of thinking that my body isn't good enough, pretty enough, or thin enough. When I was younger, I wanted my body to change so desperately that I pushed myself through long workouts and ate as little as possible. Eventually, my body couldn't function properly: I couldn't stay warm. I couldn't sleep. I had little energy. I lost my period. Even my bones weakened. Deeply concerned, my loved ones gave me a choice: I could either start eating more and exercising less, or I could go to the hospital so doctors could monitor my body and give me the nutrition I needed.

Although these physical problems were painful and even dangerous, the struggle inside was worse. The journals from my teen years reveal the daily battle in my mind: *I hate myself. Why is my body so hard to control? If I was godly, I would have more discipline. I'll never look as pretty as she does. I overeat all the time—what is wrong with me?!* I thought the visible part of me, my body, needed to change in order for the pain in my soul to get better.

But my focus slowly changed as I embraced what God's Word told me: *Our souls can't be healed by changing our bodies.* As I came to believe this truth, I came to see that God, not my body, is the only source of hope and joy.

Because God is the author behind everything you read in the Bible, it is filled with powerful messages for you today. It has the wisdom you need to navigate your struggles with your body and to experience peace in your soul. You can experience a transformation that has nothing to do with losing weight, toning your muscles, clearing your skin, or having cosmetic surgery.

Let me give you an example of how God's Word can help you. A long time ago, some teachers were telling Christians that, if they wanted to really be close to God and to gain others' approval, they needed to be harsh with their bodies. These teachers insisted that Christians needed to follow a lot of food rules and strictly regulate their bodies because these practices would earn them God's favor (Colossians 2:18–23). But they were wrong. A wise pastor named Paul wrote a letter in the Bible to set believers free from these harmful ideas. He wrote, "See to it that no one takes you captive by philosophy and empty deceit, according to human tradition . . . and not according to Christ" (Colossians 2:8). God's favor is lavished on us through Jesus Christ. It isn't earned by how we treat our bodies or by what our bodies look like. Because of Jesus's perfect life, sacrificial death, and astounding resurrection, we can receive God's grace and be reconciled to our heavenly Father when we repent of our sins and believe in him.

So how do we avoid being taken captive by bad ideas about our bodies? Like a thief, our thoughts about how we look steal our attention. They roam through our minds and snatch our focus when we could be enjoying time with family, learning a new skill, or thinking of ways to serve others. God gives us all the tools we need to resist this thief and to experience peace, hope, and freedom.

God has good purposes for our bodies. He sent Jesus to earth in a physical body as our Savior. And as our Redeemer, Jesus strengthens us to fight this battle—and he actually fights for us. We must participate in the battle, but the power and wisdom to fight come from our gracious God. He loves us and is eager to help us walk a new path.

So let's imagine the future that God holds out to you. What would it be like to have a conversation with a friend and not be worried about how your stomach looks? To take a picture without lamenting over your pose? To go to the beach and be more focused on the beauty of the ocean than on how you look in a swimsuit? To meet someone new and not plunge into despair because she is thinner, prettier, or more stylish than you? To refuse to use your body as a way to get approval, acceptance, or praise? I want you to imagine this because it's possible. It's possible because counsel from your loving heavenly Father can change your perspective on your body. When your perspective changes, you will be able to appreciate the good gift of your body while focusing more intently on your greatest treasure, the Lord Jesus.

MADE BY GOD

Bring my sons from afar and my daughters from the end of the earth, everyone who is called by my name, whom I created for my glory, whom I formed and made. (Isaiah 43:6–7)

It's time to walk a new path in our struggle with body image—keeping our steps steady with God's truth. We start with the stunning reminder that we are created *by* God and *for* God. He lovingly made us, and he has designed us to reflect the beauty of who he is.

When you pause to think that God made you, you'll notice several things. First, God designed you to have a body. Your body's complexity and intricacy came from God's mind. He created you with care and purpose. It's possible to look at your body with awe while you appreciate God as your Creator.

Not only has God created you, but, if you have trusted in Jesus, he has called you by his own name All those who are called by God's name are part of his family. We identify with him and he with us. We represent him. When we become followers of Jesus, we have a new ability to make our desires and actions more like his. That means we treat our bodies in ways that show that we belong to God. We use our bodies to love and serve others. We steward our bodies to show that they are a gift from God. We enjoy the ways we experience God's goodness through our bodies.

Being called by God's name points us to the very reason we exist. God created us as his image bearers so that we would bring him glory. God made us so that when others see how we treat our bodies and how we use them, they see true and lovely things about God. They see women who appreciate their bodies as good gifts, use their bodies to bless others, and proclaim with their voices the good news of God's salvation.

Knowing we are *made by God* is the start of it all.

POUR OUT YOUR HEART TO GOD

Trust in him at all times, O people; pour out your heart before him; God is a refuge for us. (Psalm 62:8)

Have your feelings ever put so much pressure on you that you thought you might explode? Your chest burns, your stomach aches, your head pounds. In your struggle with body image, you may have experienced anxiety, distress, a sense of inadequacy, and even despair. These emotions are hard to know how to handle. If we tell others about our struggle, we may feel misunderstood or ashamed. If we keep our feelings to ourselves, our suffering is heavier because we feel alone.

But God invites us to speak with him. In fact, he tells us to pour out everything that's inside us and promises that he will hear us with tenderness and mercy. He wants to hear what's going on in our hearts. Even if our words sound messy and frantic, he made us to communicate with him.

God welcomes our honesty when we're in pain. He is our refuge (Psalm 46:1–2): the safe place where we can wrestle with our desires and thoughts and feelings about our bodies. Through all our changing emotions, God is unchanging. He is stable and trustworthy. He always has the time and energy to help us. We can pour out our hearts to him any time without fearing his indifference or irritation.

Being honest with God about our thoughts and feelings is how he designed us to process difficult emotions. It's also the first step toward finding comfort and hope when we are desperate. During the worst of my body-image struggles, I opened my heart to the Lord through journaling. Writing helped me to slow down, to take one thought at a time, and to discover connections between my pain and God's character. Here are a few of the ways I cried out to God: *Why can't I change how I feel about my body? God, why did you make me like this? I'm worthless. Nothing about me is lovable or attractive.*

In the midst of my pain, God's promises became more precious to me. God reminded me that he is committed to changing me in every way that's needed (Philippians 1:6), including making me able to appreciate my body and steward it well. He promises to renew my mind with truth so that my thoughts and emotions reflect his wisdom and peace (Isaiah 26:3). He encourages me that my body is designed to accomplish every purpose he has for me (John 9:3).

Are you willing to pour out your heart to God? It takes energy and courage. But your loving Father waits to hear everything you share. You are safe when you express your heart to him.

Here are some ways you can get started. You might want to journal, writing down each thought as it comes. You might read a psalm and turn it into your own prayer, letting the verses shape how you talk to God. You can speak to God out loud in prayer, pushing yourself to keep talking until you've fully expressed your turmoil. It may feel awkward at first, but, as you continue, you'll treasure being able to share your heart with your loving heavenly Father.

Pray: Lord, thank you for inviting me to trust you. Please help me pour out my heart to you and seek you as my refuge, especially when I'm unhappy with my body.

Reflect: What keeps you from talking to God about your body? Have you tried, but it didn't help or nothing changed? Share these struggles with God. Then share them with a godly woman who is older than you and ask her to pray with you.

CREATED IN GOD'S IMAGE

*God created man in his own image, in the image of God he
created him; male and female he created them. (Genesis 1:27)*

Sometimes we are afraid to trust what God says and to obey what
he commands because we think he doesn't care about physical
beauty. We might think, *If I listen to God, I'll be fat and dumpy.
What if I can't achieve my ideal body* and *follow God?* The truth is
that God cares about your body and about beauty more than you
can imagine. As the Creator of everything beautiful, he knows
what true beauty is. His definition extends beyond a flawless com-
plexion or a skinny waist. He created you to possess a beauty that
transcends culture, time, and the changing opinions of others.

God cares about beauty so much that he created you to "image"
him: to represent, reflect, and display what he is like.

God designed our physical bodies to communicate spiritual
realities. Since he is the most beautiful being in the universe, and
since we have been made in his image and redeemed by Jesus, we
can be confident that we are destined for beauty.[1] We can be tiny
pictures that show something about who God is. Every person
shares the opportunity to show who God is. It's why God created
us in the first place. Not only can we experience God's goodness
through our physical senses, we can also extend God's goodness
to others by using our hands to serve, our mouths to encourage,
our ears to listen, our eyes to acknowledge, and our legs to take us
where we are needed.

Sadly, we don't think about our bodies this way. We have turned
away from God and rejected him, and our bodies and souls show
the effects of that choice. We define beauty according to our own
standards and then try to meet those standards with our own
effort. We mistakenly imagine that we need to work hard to make
ourselves acceptable to God and others. In this process, we ignore

God's words to us. When God announces that we bear his image, he offers us the relief of shifting our focus away from ourselves and our performance.

The best way to redirect our attention is to look at Jesus. He is the perfect image of God because he *is* God (Hebrews 1:3). Jesus shows us what it looks like for us to perfectly fulfill our purpose as image bearers. But we need more than a good example. We also need Jesus to be our Savior, to make us spiritually alive and able to follow him—and he does. He calls us to a far greater beauty than what the world praises, and he gives us the means to achieve it by his Holy Spirit (Romans 8:29–30).

We can be honest with God and acknowledge that we often think external attractiveness is better than the beauty of being an image bearer. As God helps us see the beauty of bearing his image, we won't be dominated by a pursuit of physical beauty. We will experience the wonder of using our bodies in a way that reflects who God is.

Pray: Dear Father, I'm amazed that I have the privilege of being made to bear your image. Thank you for the Lord Jesus, who saved me and enables me to grow in the beauty that you intend.

Act: God sees your body-image struggles, and he cares about you. He has compassion for you and wants to give you hope. When you cling to God and his purposes, he assures you that you will always be able to display his brand of beauty. Read John 9:1–41. Meditate on verse 3.

A GOOD GIFT

*The Lord God formed the man of dust from the ground
and breathed into his nostrils the breath of life, and
the man became a living creature. (Genesis 2:7)*

*And God saw everything that he had made, and
behold, it was very good. (Genesis 1:31)*

A bulging tummy. Big thighs. A flat chest. Limp hair. Acne scars. *Too tall, too short, too much here, not enough there.* When you stand in front of the mirror, do you pinch and poke yourself, disgusted by what you see and vowing to make drastic changes? Most people who struggle with body image have a list of the things they wish they could change. What's on your list? I used to want to change almost everything about my body. I viewed my body not as a gift but as an enemy. But God invites us to see our bodies differently.

When God created human beings, he gave us bodies as an act of his power and creativity. He crafted every part of our bodies—our arms, legs, brains, eyes—with loving care. Your body is a good gift that he designed to fulfill many important purposes.

That might be hard for you to believe if you've heard cruel comments about your appearance from family members or people at school. Our bodies don't seem good when they don't cooperate with us or when we can't conform them to our ideal of beauty. Many voices in our lives tell us our bodies are good only if they look a certain way, and we think we have value only if our bodies meet certain standards. But God *designed* you to have a body, and he says your body is good even if you feel disappointed with it.

As we see in our reading today, when God finished creating Adam and Eve, he proclaimed them "very good." The Bible doesn't tell us the sizes, measurements, or shapes of their bodies. They were good because they were God's.

God is pleased that you exist as an embodied being—not because you are sinless or perfect but because he designed you with physical capacities to help you know and worship him. He has given you a body with which to experience him and the world he created and with which to love and serve others. It might be hard to agree with God's description of your body if you think "good" means flawless. But God's declaration of the goodness of creation extends to you. Even when people around us—or our own thoughts—make it hard for us to believe God's Word, God's Spirit will help us to trust his voice more than what others say.

Pray: Lord, thank you for the body you've given to me. Help me see it as a gift from you so I can worship you more fully.

Reflect: Read John 1:14. Jesus, the Word of God, became a human being with a physical body. How might thinking about the fact that Jesus has a body help you embrace God's physical design for you?

CRAFTED WITH CARE

I praise you, for I am fearfully and wonderfully made. . . . Your eyes saw my unformed substance; in your book were written, every one of them, the days that were formed for me. (Psalm 139:14, 16)

When you read the words of this verse, do you scoff or roll your eyes? Do you think of words like *ugly*, *fat*, or *gross* to describe your body instead?

Have you ever tried to calm your body fears by posting your best pictures on social media? You fret as you wait for someone to reassure you. But when only your best friend likes your post or no one comments at all, your fears seem confirmed.

When you don't feel noticed by others, you might imagine that your body is the problem. And scrolling through pictures of people who seem to have perfect bodies just makes you more disgusted with yourself. Maybe you don't bother to post because you've already judged yourself. You can't measure up.

When the psalmist David thought about his body, he was amazed at God's creativity and craftsmanship. Our bodies aren't perfect, so it can be hard to think of them as marvelous. But David didn't get distracted by imperfections. Instead, he focused on the wonder of God's detailed design. Studying our bodies can spark some of this wonder.[1]

Did you know humans can detect one trillion smells?[2]

Did you know our stomach acid is strong enough to dissolve metal?[3]

Did you know one eye consists of two million working parts?[4]

Your body really is wonderfully made. God is the ultimate Artist. Even before you were born, he had planned your body's unique features, strengths, and limitations. God gave you a body for the specific plans he has for you. Nothing about your body shocks or horrifies him. He isn't repulsed when he looks at you. He sees a beloved daughter who is struggling and needs to hear his life-giving perspective.

Don't let your body frustrations cause you to miss how much you can do or cause you to underestimate the purposes God has for you. God can help you receive your body with wonder and thankfulness. Consider all the things your body can enjoy, experience, and accomplish—does that make you want to praise God? I began to see my body differently when I thanked God for arms that could give hugs, for legs that could move me where I wanted to go, and for a mouth that could detect delightful textures and flavors. Your body is not an accident or a mistake but the skillful, loving work of God. Your perspective will change as you practice thanking him for the body he has given you.

Pray: Lord, thank you for the things my body can do. Help me see the wonder of how you made my body and trust you to use my body for your wonderful purposes.

Reflect: Read Psalm 139. Take a moment to praise God for his care and creativity.

EXPERIENCING GOD'S GOODNESS

Oh, taste and see that the Lord is good! Blessed is the
[person] who takes refuge in him! (Psalm 34:8)

There was a time when I thought that if I were thin, life would be good. I exercised hard, paid attention to food labels, followed fitness accounts, counted calories, weighed myself often, and studied how influencers looked. Waves of panic engulfed me every time I didn't measure up. I was trying to create a good life by pursuing a "beautiful" body.

My definition of *good* was too narrow. God designed our bodies to experience his goodness and to extend his goodness to others. To understand and receive this goodness, we need spiritual input. We need to know that God created us as *embodied souls*—a unity of body and spirit. The physical expresses the invisible. When we blush, our bodies reveal a feeling we have in our souls. When we cry, our tears show that something is going on in our hearts. When we speak, our mouths express a thought or desire from our inner person.

Our verse today encourages us to use our physical senses to appreciate God's goodness to us. This is one reason that food tastes good—so we can understand how satisfying God is. When we taste and see God's goodness, it makes sense for us to turn to him for the comfort and peace that comes when we depend on him and listen to him. When we take refuge in God in this way, we can stop seeking refuge in a beautiful body, thinking that physical changes will bring lasting good into our lives. Our bodies can't bring us peace, but God can.

A woman named Evelyn Brand shows how beautiful we are when we experience God's goodness and share it with others. Evelyn was born to a wealthy English family in 1879. After she came to faith in Christ, she spent most of her life as a missionary in India, serving in a mountainous region that was infamous for its sickness and poverty. For the last twenty years of her life, she removed all the mirrors in her home. She didn't want her appearance to distract her from experiencing and giving God's goodness.

Although Evelyn's body weakened and wrinkled as she aged, she rejoiced that she could bring medicine, food, and hope to people in need. When she died at age ninety-five, her son said, "With wrinkles as deep and extensive as any I have ever seen on a human face, she was a beautiful woman."[1] She appreciated the body God gave her, and she used it to extend God's goodness to others.

When we nourish our inner person with God's Word, the Holy Spirit changes the way we think about and use our bodies. His grace enables us to stop fixating on our own and others' appearances and to start making friends instead. He helps us relish God's gifts to us and his purposes for us instead of getting upset over our weight, our skin, or our hair. He empowers us to stop obsessing about what others think of us and to start looking for ways to encourage them instead.

Pray: God, thank you for giving me a body that can experience your goodness. Help me take refuge in you by looking to your Word for the wisdom I need to appreciate and use my body for your purposes.

Act: Seek out a godly older woman who models the qualities in Titus 2:3–5 and ask her what she treasures most about God right now. How does she see God's goodness to her?

GOD'S GIFT OF GENDER

[Jesus] answered, "Have you not read that he who created them from the beginning made them male and female?" (Matthew 19:4)

Maria stared at the mirror, gulping back tears. She ached with confusion and anger. Everything about her body seemed like a problem: Her hair was greasy, and her face kept breaking out. Her butt and belly and breasts were all growing, and she despised the changes. *I hate the weight I've gained. I feel huge. I don't even know who I am anymore. I feel so weird.*

Your body goes through big changes during your teen years. These changes sometimes prompt questions about identity. *Why do I feel so awkward and uncomfortable in my body? Does feeling weird in my body mean I'm abnormal? Is this what being a woman feels like?*

These questions can be painful and confusing, even frightening. And you are looking for answers while your body is demanding attention in a dozen new ways. You may have heard people say that feeling strange in your body might mean you're actually in the *wrong* body. You may have heard that gender in particular is determined by something other than biology. But our gender isn't determined by how well we match cultural stereotypes or how we feel about our bodies. Our gender doesn't change even though we may be struggling to feel at peace with our bodies or our desires. Our gender is a gift we receive, not an identity we discover.

Because we are God's *female* image bearers, we can demonstrate his glory in uniquely feminine ways. The full biblical significance of our womanhood is more than we can tackle here, but I'll give you a taste. Your monthly cycle, the way your body is changing, and your female anatomy point to the potential God gave you to conceive and nurture new life and to help life flourish. Even if you never have biological children (like me), your body points to your role as a woman in encouraging life to thrive—wherever you find it.[1] God is the source of all life, and your female body is a reflection of his creative, life-giving purposes.

For now, it's important to know that God's truth can be a life raft in the flood of confusing emotions. Whether you are asking questions about your gender or simply trying to make peace with changes in your body, God has designed you to have a physical body that is female.

Peace comes from trusting God and believing he didn't make a mistake when he created your biological body. This is a difficult truth to accept if someone has come to believe that gender is determined by what they like or do or desire—or that the answer to their distress is to change their body. But I want you to see that it is a great relief to have a foundation that doesn't shift. Our good God chose your gender for you when he created your body. He invites you to trust him in this area, even when you are hurting. Following our own path leads to greater confusion and isolation, but God's path leads to peace.

> **Pray:** God, please help me believe that your ways are perfect (Psalm 18:30). Help me understand and embrace the purposes you have for my female body.
>
> **Reflect:** You may have been hurt by people who rely on stereotypes more than they honor God and his ways. We all struggle to love the bodies God gave us. Sometimes that struggle includes accepting the gender God chose for you. As you pray and ask God to help you trust his design, remember that peace comes not from choosing your own path but from following God's.

LOOKING FOR BEAUTY

One thing have I asked of the LORD, that will I seek after:
that I may dwell in the house of the LORD all the days of my
life, to gaze upon the beauty of the LORD. (Psalm 27:4)

As you scroll through social media, have you ever scrutinized an influencer's latest post and thought, "How can someone look so perfect?!" It's almost automatic for us to compare ourselves to the people we follow online. But many photos that teens post on social media have been edited. This isn't a big deal when people are removing red eyes or adding some light. But more drastic photo edits create a problem: We might be comparing ourselves to faces and bodies that don't even exist. And if we edit our own photos before posting, we may feel like we can never measure up in person to the appearance we portray online. Tweaking our online appearance can fuel shame for those who are already struggling with their body image.

We naturally seek beauty. To satisfy this longing, we often turn to a mirror or a filter. But what we see disappoints us, even on our best days. The author of our verse today, King David, had discovered where to find soul-satisfying beauty—and it's not where we would expect. He longed to gaze on God's beauty.

How do we look at the beauty of someone who is invisible? It takes more than physical sight. We have to use the "eyes of [our] hearts" (Ephesians 1:18). That's the way we recognize the beauty of kindness, compassion, or mercy. Gazing on the beauty of the Lord means using our minds to contemplate how amazing God is and to think about his character and savor it like a bite of delicious food.

Do you think of God as beautiful? When David concentrated on God's beauty, he described him as powerful and faithful; he called him his light, his salvation, and his stronghold. David could see this beauty because he had studied God's Word and had seen

God's character in action. God had helped David when his enemies attacked him, when they lied about him, and when they tried to destroy his reputation and even his life. Psalm 27 describes it all. Knowing David's circumstances makes his focus on God even more amazing. David could have been focused on the bad things that had happened to him or consumed with his own appearance, skills, or performance as he tried to protect himself. Instead, God's loveliness and power filled his mind.

When we're struggling with our body image, we need to understand God's beauty the way David did. We're easily obsessed with trying to enhance our own beauty. We think we'll be happy if we're physically beautiful. But our definition of beauty is mixed up. We can learn from David, who recognized the ultimate beauty of the invisible God and was captivated by it.

Looking at ourselves or at others will never satisfy us. Even if we attain a measure of external beauty, it won't last, and it won't fulfill us. God designed us to look at him and to dwell in his presence.

Pray: Lord God, I'm glad I get to see your beauty. Please transform and redeem my view of my body as I gaze at you.

Act: Read Psalm 27. Ask God to give you eyes to see his beauty.

WORSHIP GOD WITH YOUR BODY

*I appeal to you therefore, brothers and sisters, by the mercies
of God, to present your bodies as a living sacrifice, holy and
acceptable to God, which is your spiritual worship. (Romans 12:1)*

As a biblical counselor, I work to help people discover connections, like the connection between body image and worship. Since the most common thing women dislike about their bodies is their weight, that's often where we start. Say a woman I am counseling makes a general statement: *I need to lose weight.* I then ask her a series of questions. These questions aren't meant to annoy her but meant to help us both understand what's connected to her struggle with her body. So I ask, "Why do you want to lose weight?" *If I lose weight, I'll fit into my new dress.* "Why does that matter?" *Because if I fit into this dress, I'll look good for the party.* "Why is that important?" *Because I want to be admired by the people who'll be there.* "Why?" *Because it feels good to be praised. When people pay attention to me and approve of me, it seems like my life matters and that I belong.*

With just a few questions, we have discovered a connection between body image and *worship*—the act of loving and assigning worth to something.

This example might not capture your own thoughts. But I hope you can trace its logic. Any desire you have to change your body connects back to something you want and value. When you keep asking yourself "Why?" you'll eventually be able to discover what your heart worships.

The person in the example above values the praise and approval of others. Her worship guides her choices: She wants to lose weight so that she can be accepted and praised. Other people want to have well-defined muscles because they value feeling powerful or tough. Others crave the sense of achievement and pride that comes from being the thinnest or most fashionable person in the room. Some people even consider cosmetic surgery in hope of earning affirmation and love. Even though what you want to change is unique to you, the root issue is about worship.

In our verse today, the apostle Paul urges us to worship God with our bodies. That means we need to use our bodies to express our devotion to God. It also means that any time we consider making changes to our bodies, we need to start with God and his purposes for us instead of starting with the assumption that we need a physical "fix" to give us meaning or worth.

As we read God's Word, think about our hearts, and speak to caring people in our lives, the Holy Spirit can help us detect what we are worshiping. He and others can help us use biblical principles to evaluate whether we need to change our eating or exercise habits. We can then make decisions about our bodies from a place of worship, not panic. As we meditate on God's many mercies to us, we can rejoice in using our bodies not as objects to achieve status or love but as instruments to enjoy God and serve others.

Pray: Heavenly Father, please help me to love you with all of who I am. Please transform what I treasure so I can worship you fully as a living sacrifice.

Act: Look up Matthew 22:37–39. What are two ways you can express your wholehearted love to God today?

BROKEN BY SIN

So when the woman saw that the tree was good for food, and that it was a delight to the eyes, and that the tree was to be desired to make one wise, she took of its fruit and ate, and she also gave some to her husband who was with her, and he ate. (Genesis 3:6)

When we struggle with our body image, it's helpful for us to grasp the bigger picture: Something has gone wrong in us and in the world. The first people whom God created, Adam and Eve, disobeyed him and ate from the one tree he had forbidden to them. The Bible calls their disobedience *sin*, which is to fail to love and obey God in the ways he commands. Not only do we inherit their sin nature, but we also make the same decision to doubt and disobey God. Just as it did for Adam and Eve, our sin separates us from God, brings us under his judgment, and breaks down our relationship with him.

When sin ruptured our connection to God, a cascade of problems followed. Although sin affects us in lots of ways, three in particular help us understand our struggles with body image.

First, Adam and Eve's first sin had consequences for the whole world. We get sick, we get injured, we age, and eventually we die. We are born with disabilities or lose abilities over time. Our bodies, like the rest of the world, groan for God's redemption (Romans 8:20–23).

Second, our bodies experience other people's sin. Others don't love and care for us according to God's high standards. When they break God's law, they inflict misery and pain. They speak cruel words about our appearance, reject and condemn us because of how we look, and commit acts of physical or sexual abuse (Psalms 56:1–7; 59:1–7; 64:1–6). This brings suffering into our lives.

The third way sin affects us has to do with our own hearts. Unless God intervenes to change our hearts, we worship created things rather than him. The Bible calls this idolatry. Remember what we saw on day 8? What we worship affects how we think. When our hearts worship idols, our feelings and thoughts about our bodies become disordered as we start thinking about our bodies based on our ideas instead of God's. Rather than enjoying our bodies as a good gift to glorify God and love others, we evaluate our bodies based on whether they give us meaning and acceptance on our own terms (Romans 1:21–25).

In this section, we'll see how our own sin and the sin of others against us affect our perspective on our bodies. We'll also see the hope that the Lord Jesus offers us.

SIN IS UGLY

*All have sinned and fall short of the glory of God,
and are justified by his grace as a gift, through the
redemption that is in Christ Jesus. (Romans 3:23–24)*

I sometimes wonder what would happen if my sin were made visible. What if everyone could see my pride, envy, anger, or self-ishness? Even though I know these things are bad and I should deal with them, I'm tempted to focus on what others can see, like acne, extra weight, thin hair, or unfashionable clothes. Maybe I focus on improving or hiding my appearance because changing my sinful habits seems impossible. Or because I think outward alterations will please others. Or because I want to be praised more than I want to play my part in God's story.

Our upbringings, our cultures, our personalities, and our unique physical characteristics all influence the way we try to fix our bodies. Different people express the same longing for approval, or fear of rejection, or desire to be loved, in different ways. One person might eat very little in an attempt to disappear, while someone else might gain weight to protect herself from leering looks. Someone might wear baggy clothes to hide her body so no one will judge her. Someone else might bare some skin, thinking that if enough people see and approve, she'll feel okay about herself.

Efforts to improve our appearance aren't wrong, but they can distract us from the real problem. Without God's Word to guide us, we don't know that our biggest problem is our sin—not how we look. Sin separates us from God and brings us under his judgment.

God gives us clarity about sin so we can't wriggle away from his conviction. We have betrayed God by forsaking him—our holy Creator—the kindest, most loving, most generous person in the universe. We have rejected God by denying his care, guidance, authority, and wisdom. We have ignored God, questioning why he matters or why we should give him our attention, affection, or obedience. In these ways and more, we have fallen short of cherishing God and living for his glory.

Because sin separates us from God, our ultimate need is to be made right with him. The good news of the gospel is that God makes that possible. When we see the ugliness in our hearts and ask God to forgive us, today's verse tells us how he responds: He shows us mercy. His Son, Jesus, the promised King, took the punishment our sins deserved and rose from the dead, defeating death itself. Our only hope is to come to this God and be made right with him—not through our efforts but through faith in Jesus (Romans 3:28). When we ask God to forgive us for ignoring and rejecting him, he will cleanse us on the basis of Jesus's life, death, and resurrection. He will make us truly beautiful.

Pray: God, thank you for telling me what my biggest problem is and for sending Jesus to be my Savior. Please help me treasure you and your glory above everything else.

Reflect: Are you trying to fix your body to solve a problem that is much deeper? Do you long to know the truth about yourself and about God?

Day 10

EXPOSED TO SHAME

Then the eyes of both were opened, and they knew that they were naked. And they sewed fig leaves together and made themselves loincloths. (Genesis 3:7)

Joanne struggled through tears to get the story out. Some boys in her high school had rigged a camera in one of the locker rooms—the room she always used. When she found out, she could barely process it. Anger and shame flooded her as she started to evaluate her body from the perspective of the guys behind the camera. She felt exposed and ridiculed, even though she hadn't done anything wrong. She couldn't explain why, but she felt dirty and worthless.[1]

Sometimes we feel shame because we have sinned—we know God sees us and the wrong things we have done. But other times we feel shame because others have sinned against us: Like the boys with Joanne, they have taken advantage of us and used us for evil purposes. God graciously speaks to both kinds of shame throughout the Bible.

Humanity's experience of shame begins with Adam and Eve. When they disobeyed God, their relationship with him changed—and so did how they thought about their bodies. Suddenly they were aware of their bodies in a painful way they had never known before. And here's the thing: Their *bodies* hadn't changed, only their perception of them. In sin and shame, they wanted to cover themselves and hide.

Not only do we inherit their shame, but our own sin adds to our shame—and then others pile on more shame as they sin against us. We may focus our shame on our bodies, thinking they are the problem. But the story of Adam and Eve reminds us that the problem goes deeper. Shame pushes us to find ways to cover ourselves and hide. Even when we can't pinpoint the sources of our shame, we feel unacceptable and exposed.

God has a solution that deals abundantly with our shame, no matter its source. He gives us a covering—a "robe of righteousness" (Isaiah 61:10)—that shows we are reconciled to him despite our flaws and others' mistreatment of us (Psalm 3:3; Romans 5:1; 1 Corinthians 1:30). It is a solution to shame that only he can provide, and it allows us to reject the shame that others put on us.

When we put our trust in Christ instead of trying to hide, God exchanges our sin and shame for this glorious and beautiful covering. This robe symbolizes our salvation and adoption into God's family. It means that, in God's eyes, our sin has been covered by Jesus's perfection. Any shame put on us by others is now blanketed with his love and acceptance. Because we wear this robe, we can stop fixating on our bodies, hating ourselves when we don't look the way we want, or feeling dirty or disgusting because others have misused us. We can stop viewing our bodies as sources of pain and shame and start experiencing God's goodness through them and extending it to others.

The good news of the gospel is that God deals with sin in every way it affects us, even when that sin is not our own. Jesus suffered in our place when he bore the full wrath of God and the shame of our sin on the cross (1 Peter 2:24). In making us right with God, he covers the shame we experience, whatever its source (Romans 3:22–25).

Sometimes we forget we are wearing a beautiful robe. We feel naked and exposed to judging eyes—our own or others'. But we wear costly spiritual clothes that represent God's protection and our nearness to him. What a comfort!

Pray: Lord, your salvation is amazing. You deal with my sin, and you cover the shame I feel when others sin against me. Help me remember the beautiful spiritual clothes that I wear.

Act: Read Isaiah 61. Write down or say out loud the amazing ways God tells us he will bless his people.

FREEDOM FROM CONDEMNATION

*There is therefore now no condemnation for those
who are in Christ Jesus. (Romans 8:1)*

Allison huddled against her bedroom wall, sobbing. She could barely breathe as she thought back to her swim meet earlier that day. When she walked onto the pool deck, one girl nudged her friend and said loudly, "Here comes the whale!" Another girl chimed in: "We could win some races if the whale wasn't dragging an extra thirty pounds with her!" Allison couldn't imagine going back to school after that day, and she vowed never to go near another swimming pool.

Condemnation has many sources. Sometimes we are our own worst critics, keeping a running list of the things we hate about our bodies. But sometimes we get cruel words dumped on us by the people near us—classmates and teammates or even parents and coaches. One heartless comment can make us hyperalert as we try to protect ourselves from future attacks.

When you are struggling with your body image, you may constantly feel condemned and worthless. To keep from being sucked under by the negativity within you and around you, you need to be firmly rooted "in Christ Jesus." If you are in Christ Jesus, that means that God has drawn you to himself in love and saved you by giving you the ability to repent and believe in him. When you are in Christ Jesus, you are no longer separated from God and ruled by sin. Instead, the Holy Spirit lives within you to lavish God's love on you and to help you live like Jesus.

When others belittle or humiliate you, remind yourself that God has united you to Jesus. Other people may sin against you with their attitudes and words, but they don't have the power to change your standing with God. God has *justified* you—meaning that because Jesus endured the punishment you deserve for your sin, you will never be condemned in God's court of justice. God's forgiveness is based not on you, your performance, your body, or the evaluation of others but on the work of his Son. You are secure because of your perfect Savior.

What's more, your right standing with God gives you the foundation you need to withstand the accusations and scorn of others. It hurts when others sin against you, like when Allison's teammates made unkind comments about her body. But what you tell yourself when others attack you makes a huge difference. Try speaking these truths to yourself: *God chose this body for me (Jeremiah 1:5). It's a wonderful gift, created for good works (Ephesians 2:10). I'm doing the best I can with what I have. I refuse to treat these cruel words as though they're more important than they are (Galatians 1:10). God is pleased with my body even if others aren't (Psalm 139:13–15). His evaluation is more important than theirs (1 Corinthians 4:3–4).*

Jesus gives you comfort and hope when others hurt you. He will never leave you or stop helping you. The world doesn't recognize the beauty of following God and being full of the Holy Spirit. But this beauty is real, and it shines from those who are "in Christ."

Pray: Heavenly Father, thank you for comforting me when others sin against me. Help me hear your voice over the voice of my critics.

Act: Read Romans 8 and write down at least two verses that help you focus on God's goodness and give you hope.

Day 12

SQUEEZED BY LIES

Do not be conformed to this world, but be transformed by the renewal of your mind, that by testing you may discern what is the will of God, what is good and acceptable and perfect. (Romans 12:2)

Have you ever tried to shimmy into a dress, only to have it get stuck at your armpits? I have. Undeterred by the warning signs, I pulled the dress down over my body. The dress squeezed my chest, my tummy, and my hips. Not only was it unflattering, it was downright uncomfortable. I couldn't take a deep breath, and I couldn't move freely. I peeled the dress off as quickly as I could with a gasp of relief.

The world can spiritually squeeze us in uncomfortable—and even dangerous—ways too. That's why the apostle Paul wrote this verse. He wanted to spare us the suffocating squeeze of the world's agenda for our lives and our bodies.

The world around us does not believe that God is good. It ignores him and seeks to make its own definitions of what is good and beautiful. Because the world misunderstands and contradicts God, it cannot correctly understand and interpret life. Instead it creates a mold of half-truths and downright lies and tries to squeeze us into it.

We need to recognize the lies that we have embraced or are tempted to live by. Do you sometimes repeat any of the following lies? *I'm not special if I'm not good-looking. Only attractive people have good relationships and successful lives. How I look proves whether I'm a worthwhile person. My happiness depends on my body. I can be happy only if I like my body.* How do these kinds of thoughts shape your mood and behavior?

The world repeats its lies in lots of ways: through music, social media, movies, TV shows—even through our friends and role models. Even though we might acknowledge that these ideas are

39

lies, they are still hard to dismiss. We too may begin to doubt that God is good and has good plans for us. That's why we need to filter everything through his Word and to depend on the power of the Holy Spirit to renew our minds.

Thinking about the lies I'm tempted to believe can be overwhelming. It helps me to remember that God has promised to transform his children (Philippians 1:6). He declares that we can renew our minds. We're not stuck.

The best way to equip ourselves to recognize and defeat the world's lies is to spend time reading God's Word. Meditating on God's goodness is particularly important. God wants you to define goodness the way he does so that you can experience his goodness. That is true freedom.

Pray: Lord, you are good, but sometimes I don't recognize it. Please open the eyes of my heart so that I see your goodness and trust you more.

Reflect: Write down three lies about your body that you tend to believe. Since God transforms us when we repent, start by asking him to forgive you for replacing truth with lies. Then ask him to give you the strength to hold fast to the truth.

BODY EXPECTATIONS

Now Laban had two daughters. The name of the older was Leah, and the name of the younger was Rachel. Leah's eyes were weak, but Rachel was beautiful in form and appearance. Jacob loved Rachel. (Genesis 29:16–18)

I don't have a sister, and so it's easy for me to romanticize what having one might be like. But sisters often have tough relationships. Take Leah and Rachel, for example. Although Leah was older, she lived in the shadow of her younger sister, who was "beautiful in form and appearance." When a handsome young man named Jacob arrived in their village, Leah probably wasn't surprised when he fell in love with Rachel (Genesis 29:10). But that doesn't mean it stung any less.

Through a crazy turn of events, Rachel and Leah both ended up married to Jacob. Leah knew Jacob favored Rachel, but she was desperate for Jacob to love her too. She had no hope of winning a beauty contest with Rachel. She thought she might be able to win her husband's affection by using her body in a way that her culture would applaud—by having lots of children.

Even though she was beautiful, Rachel was also desperate. Jacob clearly favored her, but she wasn't able to have children for several years, and she felt threatened by her sister's fertility. She even told Jacob, "Give me children, or I shall die!" (Genesis 30:1). Her beauty and her husband's love didn't satisfy her. She imagined she would be more secure in her marriage if she continued to trump her sister in every way.

Both Leah and Rachel worshiped Jacob. They wanted his love and approval above all things (see day 8), and they tried to use their bodies as tools to get his affection. But their bodies couldn't deliver what they craved.

Even though we live in a different culture, we still often expect our bodies to give us success, opportunities, and good relationships. We think that a better body will get us an adoring boyfriend. We imagine that losing weight will finally make our parents proud of us. We assume that having the right clothes and makeup will make important people pay attention to us—so that we can get the scholarship we want or the job we need or the spot on the student government that will boost our résumé. We believe that if we can just get stronger and fitter, we'll be accepted by others. We may try to mask our gender or find ways to be invisible. Although physical beauty or ability might bring certain advantages, our bodies will never make us secure in our relationships.

The scheming between Leah and Rachel in Genesis 29 and 30 is so sad. They didn't pay attention to the ways God was blessing them. Since they were zoned in on getting Jacob's attention, God's perfect love seemed distant to them.

When we get distracted by our body expectations, God challenges us to focus instead on his remarkable care for us. When we do this, we begin to see that what we most need is not the affection of others but the love of God that is poured out on us when we are reconciled to him in Christ. With that change of perspective, we can stop expecting our bodies to provide what only God himself can.

Pray: God, I want to appreciate your care more fully and, knowing your love, I want to love you and others more. Please forgive me for treasuring the love and approval of others above you.

Reflect: What are you hoping to change about your body? What do you think those changes will accomplish in your life?

DESPERATE FOR CONTROL

*For freedom Christ has set us free; stand firm therefore, and
do not submit again to a yoke of slavery. (Galatians 5:1)*

We all have unique stories of how we battle for control of our
bodies and where our battles lead us. I used to be part of a group
of teenage girls who shared our struggles with one another. One
girl had been arrested for stealing laxatives. Another girl had piles
of jeans of all sizes to fit her frequently changing body throughout cycles of binging. Another was so malnourished that fine,
downy hair covered her body. Someone else had esophagus dam-
age and rotting teeth due to purging. Even though we had different backgrounds, we all shared a common misery.

Their stories were heartbreaking. They shared about their parents' divorces, cruel classmates, abuse by family members, and
abandonment by boyfriends who had used them sexually. They
longed to feel powerful, like they could protect themselves, like
they could do something to avoid more suffering. In deep pain,
they turned their energy to something they could control: their
bodies. They slowly formulated lots of rules in order to achieve
the bodies they thought could give them the security they craved.

Do you have a list of rules that helps you feel in control? Maybe
you have a list of low-calorie "safe" foods. Perhaps you have a rule
about how long and how hard you will exercise. Do you feel sad
or anxious when you break one of your rules?

Instead of giving us more rules to follow, our verse today offers
good news about what Jesus has done to set us free. The apostle
Paul wrote to the Galatians because they thought they had to do
something painful and permanent to their bodies (be circumcised)
in order to get right with God. But their rules about their bodies
actually *separated* them from God. Relying on Jesus alone for salvation seemed scary.[1] They wanted to add an outward, physical sign

that they could control. But their rules jeopardized the freedom Christ came to give them. Our rules are the same: They can't save us, and they aren't the solution for gaining control over our messy, painful lives.

We try to maintain control by making rules about our bodies, but that is not the path of our Savior. Our verse reminds us that Christ has set us free—free from depending on ourselves for safety and security. Free from focusing on our bodies as the way to manage our lives. Free from using our own rules to prove our value. Free from experiencing God's wrath when we try to be our own saviors. Free to rest in God's control over our lives.

Embracing your freedom in Christ is very practical. Freedom might mean gratefully accepting the food you are served instead of anxiously looking for a lower-calorie option. Freedom might mean choosing to eat with others instead of eating alone to hide your food habits. Freedom might mean loving your family by making breakfast with your mom instead of rushing to the gym to get your workout in. The freedom God gives is better than the tyranny of striving for control.

Pray: Lord, thank you for the freedom and grace you give. Help me believe in your love and walk in your ways.

Reflect: List some rules you have around eating or exercising. What benefits do the rules promise to deliver?

ENVY KILLS JOY

If we live by the Spirit, let us also keep in step with the
Spirit. Let us not become conceited, provoking one
another, envying one another. (Galatians 5:25–26)

Aisha tried not to stare as Stella started her second doughnut. Stella could eat whatever she wanted and stay thin. Aisha couldn't remember the last time she'd had a doughnut, or a slice of cake, or even bread. Beside Stella, Monique seemed to glow, the light from the window highlighting her perfectly clear skin and long thick hair. Aisha dropped her eyes as a familiar sense of sadness and defeat welled up in her heart. The more she thought about her friends' advantages, the worse she felt. It was hard for her to be thankful and content. Something was eating up her joy.

Envy is the discontent we feel when someone receives attention and praise for something we wish we had. Envy recognizes that someone else is glorious in a way we aren't and dislikes them for it. And that feeling kills our joy and stirs up strife in our hearts.[1] We don't want to be near the people we envy, and we stop enjoying the gifts we do possess.

Envy starts with comparison. Making a comparison is not inherently wrong—God tells us it's good for us to imitate the godliness of others (Hebrews 6:12). But comparing our own bodies to other people's is another story. We make those kinds of comparisons when we're seeking glory for ourselves, and it usually leads straight to misery. We determine we don't measure up. Someone else is prettier, thinner, stronger, healthier, more stylish, or more at ease with her body. We hate that this other person has something we don't.

But God has given us a way out of this misery. We can *keep in step with the Spirit*. In the context of our verses for today, this means we depend on God and walk in his ways. God tells us clearly that envy is sin (Galatians 5:21), so he will help us kill it. We don't have to live with the poison of envy rotting us inside.

When I have an envy attack, I fight back with truth. Here's a short reminder that helps me: "God gets to decide." In his love and wisdom, he determined all the details of my body, including how fast my metabolism is, how tall I am, how clear my skin is, and how much money I have to spend on clothes or makeup or gym fees. When I focus on God and remember that his ways are perfect, my envy starts to melt. His decisions about my body are part of how he has organized all things to work together for my good and his glory (Romans 8:28). He sees the whole picture and knows what's best. He has the wisdom to know what I need, the love to give me what I need, and the power to bring it all to pass. When I keep my eyes on him, I remain focused on his love and goodness and not on what I don't have.

Pray: Father, please forgive me for wanting the body and the beauty that belong to another person. Forgive me for distrusting you. And forgive me for being unloving (even in my thoughts) because someone else has something I don't.

Act: Read Proverbs 14:30. Ask God to help you have a tranquil heart that is free from envy. Write a note of encouragement to someone you have envied and highlight something about their character that you admire. Thank God for their life and gifts.

ADDRESS SPIRALING THOUGHTS

*To set the mind on the flesh is death, but to set the
mind on the Spirit is life and peace. (Romans 8:6)*

As Meijing searched social media for healthy recipes, she found
an influencer with great meal plans. The influencer also posted
pictures of her workouts in her tiny workout clothes. Tiny workout clothes for her tiny, perfect body. After viewing a few posts,
Meijing got up to do her chores, but she felt sad and sluggish.
She couldn't pinpoint the reason. But later that night, she real-
ized that seeing the influencer had sparked a cascade of negative
thoughts. The first one was "I don't look like her." And then "I'm
so fat. I could never be as small as she is." The thoughts picked up
speed: "I need to pay more attention to my eating and exercising.
But I always fail. I will never look like her. Why even bother? I
hate myself."

Spiraling thoughts are linked to one another like stairs that
descend to a dark place. They usually start with a negative thought
("I don't look like her"). This leads to another thought that is
usually false or incomplete ("I'm so fat"). The spiral continues as
distressing emotions begin to grow within you ("I always fail").
If you don't pause to halt the spiral, you'll soon feel fearful and
hopeless ("I hate myself").

Our verse today tells us that where we set our minds makes the
difference between life and death. To set our minds on something is
to be preoccupied with it, to fill our thoughts with it, to continually
think about it and roll it over in our minds. Life and peace come
from setting our minds on the Spirit of God.

I learned how to set my mind on the Spirit by filling note cards
with Bible verses, quotations, and reminders of truth. I would read
my Bible each morning and then review a few of my cards. That was
nonnegotiable. I knew if I didn't interrupt the thought patterns I

had been weaving for years, I would not be able to bring my emotions under the Holy Spirit's control. I needed to combat the lies and hopeless thoughts with truths that were specific to my needs. I was excited to realize that I could choose what to think about. Slowly but steadily, the thoughts I had chosen began to impact my feelings. Although I wasn't transformed overnight, and I still had distressing emotions, I started to recognize the thoughts behind those emotions. Now it was time to fight them.

First, I wrote out each hopeless thought in a sentence on one side of a notecard. This had the unexpected benefit of showing me I didn't have an endless number of anxious or despairing thoughts. I had a handful that kept coming up over and over. It was helpful to see each familiar lie now nailed down on paper, no longer swirling in my mind.

Then, with the help of wise women and the Bible, I worked to come up with a short, true statement to respond to each lie. Sometimes a specific verse matched my need. Other times, I used a summary of the gospel or a quotation that catapulted me out of the spiral. I meditated on these bits of truth—not as mantras that I mindlessly repeated but as prayers to the Lord that were based on the promises in his Word. I even carried one or two with me so I could pull them out and look at them in class, on the bus, or in the locker room. Giving my attention to these truths began to fill my mind with peace. It can do the same for you.

Pray: Heavenly Father, I see how my thought spirals lead to painful feelings. Will you please help me cling to truth from your Word and set my mind on the things that you say matter most every day?

Act: Make your own note card today. Write a spiraling thought on one side and then ask the Lord to help you think about the truth that addresses it. Write that truth on the opposite side, then put the note card with your Bible so you can review it during your devotional time.

THE COMPARISON TRAP

*Who shall separate us from the love of Christ? Shall tribulation,
or distress, or persecution[?] ... I am sure that ... [nothing]
else in all creation will be able to separate us from the love
of God in Christ Jesus our Lord. (Romans 8:35, 38–39)*

As Danielle walked into the room, self-loathing thoughts flooded into her mind. She took a few deep breaths to steady herself and braced as a familiar wave of distress crashed over her: *I'm bigger than every girl here. Everyone who sees me writes me off as lazy or disgusting or a slob.*

If you have ever been the biggest girl in the room, I wonder what the hardest part of this experience was for you. Our world is cruel to those of us who don't fit a very narrow definition of beauty. Sometimes it seems like the only way to be "beautiful" by our culture's standards is to make unhealthy or unreasonable choices. God sees your suffering. And he wants you to know that he loves you. He loves you at every weight you will ever be.

God doesn't think about you the way other people do. His care doesn't vary with the number on the scale. Nothing can separate you from the love of Christ—not your body size, not the judgment of others, not your own self-hatred. God isn't ashamed to be identified with you. Even when you feel like an outcast, he pours his love on you and offers you his comfort.

If God's love doesn't seem to be making much of a difference for you right now, there could be several reasons. Is the voice of shame so loud that you struggle to hear God's loving words to you? It takes time and the work of the Holy Spirit for certain truths from Scripture to work their way into our hearts. Don't despair. Keep immersing yourself in the truth.

Maybe you think your body is the best way to assess how you are doing in life. Does your perception of your body color your whole existence? We honor God when we take good care of our bodies. But we must reject the belief that our bodies define our worth. You are an image bearer of God, and you have the ability to display God's beauty no matter what size you are.

Maybe your mind is a riot of accusing thoughts—you feel like it's your fault that you're bigger than other girls. Even if you think you could reasonably make healthy changes in your eating or exercise habits, God's love for you doesn't change. This is so important for you to know. God wants any changes you contemplate to come from a knowledge of his love, not a sense that you need to hide from him or strive to earn his—or other people's—approval. Draw near to God through prayer, and he will meet you and comfort you.

When you are overwhelmed by self-loathing, that bad feeling is an invitation for you to trust God and turn your heart to him. He wants you to find your joy in him and his salvation (Romans 4:8). You are never separated from God's love.

The fact that you can't be separated from God's love means you always have someone to share your heart with (Psalm 62:8), someone to comfort you (2 Corinthians 1:3–4), someone who doesn't despise you or sneer at you (Matthew 12:15–21), someone who helps you with great tenderness (Isaiah 49:15), someone who never stops praying for you (Hebrews 7:25).

Pray: Father, thank you for telling me who you are in your Word. I'm grateful for your comfort and help. Help me believe in your love for me.

Reflect: Maybe body size isn't your struggle. What other aspect of your body do you compare to others? What do you tend to notice about other women's bodies and wish you had?

UNITED TO CHRIST

Because of him you are in Christ Jesus, who became to us wisdom from God, righteousness and sanctification and redemption, so that, as it is written, "Let the one who boasts, boast in the Lord." (1 Corinthians 1:30–31)

When we respond to God's gift of salvation, our lives blossom as we begin to think, act, and love in new ways. Now that we are in Christ, our sins are forgiven, and we are relationally connected to our loving God and made spiritually alive. His life flows through ours with power so that we can show others what he is like.

Being united to Christ means we have a living, intimate connection to our Savior. As the church, we are the body of Christ, and Christ is our head (Ephesians 4:15–16). This means we look to him to guide our lives and to help us think like he does. Let me give you an example.

Think about someone you admire—someone you think is physically attractive. What's important to her? What does she focus on? Does she pursue lush, long eyelashes? A thigh gap? Full lips? A small waist? Because you admire her, you might find yourself valuing what she values. You think full eyelashes are a must-have. You will do whatever it takes to have a thigh gap. You think about how to plump your lips and slim your waist. Who you admire affects what you value.

When we admire God most of all, we value what God values. We want to praise the things that God says are praiseworthy. When God and his ways become most valuable to us, when we trust in him as our wisdom and righteousness, he will begin to help us find our utmost satisfaction in him. Learning to focus our attention on God instead of our bodies will be a lifelong process, but God is with us as we grow in him.

We change our perspective on our bodies by knowing and appreciating God more and more. It seems counterintuitive. It seems like we should focus on improving our bodies in order to stop hating them. But lasting change comes from changing who we worship and what we value. When we recognize that God didn't make us to worship created things (either our bodies or the way others perceive us), we can focus on worshiping him. We'll be freed to interact with our bodies as good gifts from God without demanding that they fulfill our souls as only he can. This freedom comes from being united to Christ.

YOU ARE A STEWARD

*Whether you eat or drink, or whatever you do, do
all to the glory of God. (1 Corinthians 10:31)*

Do you think about eating and drinking as opportunities for you
to bring glory to God? It might be strange to consider, but these
daily actions are things God cares about. Our verse today gives us
an important truth: We are stewards of our bodies. A steward is
someone who is entrusted to manage and cultivate something of
value on someone else's behalf. Jesus is the King who created and
redeemed us, body and soul. He has assigned us the privilege of
stewarding the bodies he gave us.

In 1 Corinthians 10, Paul talks to believers in Corinth about
how they ought to handle eating food that has been offered to
idols. He wants the Corinthians to focus on glorifying God as they
make decisions around food. Even though the idols in our culture
are different from those in ancient Corinth, the principles Paul is
teaching are important for us too.

If we are supposed to do everything to the glory of God, we
need to know what God's glory is. Here's one way to define it:
God's glory is the "truth and beauty of his character."[1] So when we
glorify God, we are highlighting how true and lovely his character
is. We are telling the truth about who he is in a way that exalts
him and helps others admire him.[2]

How we treat our bodies sends a message to others about
what we believe about God. That's why Paul says, "Glorify God in
your body" (1 Corinthians 6:20) and "Whether you eat or drink
or whatever you do, do all to the glory of God." We are actually
able to help others know God through how we interact with our
bodies. Let me give you some examples.

God loves life. So we don't do things that harm our bodies.
Since he is the creator of life, we tell the truth about God by not

hurting, mistreating, or abusing our bodies or the bodies of others (John 11:25–26).

God is generous and gives good gifts. We honor God by remembering that he provides us with every good thing (James 1:17). We tell the truth about God when we appreciate the pleasures he wants our bodies to experience, like when we eat delicious food, feel the sun on our skin, and enjoy a warm bath, a cool drink, or a tender hug.

God is our greatest joy. Even as we enjoy the pleasures God provides, we don't ask them to satisfy our souls. Only God can do that. Only God can be our exceedingly great joy (Psalm 43:4). His steadfast love is better than life—or food, or clothes, or a certain body type (Psalm 63:3).

God is our Sustainer. We cannot live by food alone (Matthew 4:4). We don't expect any created thing to provide everything we need (Psalm 73:25–26). He gives us rules and guidance so we can flourish (1 Corinthians 6:19–20).

God is our only Savior. We aren't striving to deserve or earn love with our bodies. We have security and purpose in Christ (1 Peter 2:9–10). We don't find our refuge or safety in the praise of others (Jeremiah 17:5–8).

Pray: God, you are amazing. You are my Savior and Sustainer and the Giver of everything good. Thank you giving me life now and eternally.

Act: Choose one of the ways of telling the truth about God from the reading above, and ask for his help to live it out this week.

Day 19

REAL CONFIDENCE

*I count everything as loss because of the surpassing worth
of knowing Christ Jesus my Lord. For his sake I have suffered
the loss of all things and count them as rubbish, in order
that I may gain Christ and be found in him, not having a
righteousness of my own that comes from the law, but that
which comes through faith in Christ. (Philippians 3:8–9)*

Before Paul put his trust in Christ for salvation, he based his reasons for confidence on what he had achieved in his own strength.
He wrote, "If anyone else thinks he has reason for confidence in
the flesh, I have more" (Philippians 3:4). Paul pointed to his Jew-
ish ethnicity, his efforts to be righteous, and his physical keeping
of God's law as evidence that he was on the right path. We often
look to things we can achieve with our bodies as a source of reas-
surance too.

If we are gifted athletically, we might look to our achievements
on the field or on the court or in the pool as our source of confidence. If we have musical talent or excel academically, we might
base our sense of confidence on results we can observe. People at
the top of their game often talk about the pressure they feel to
keep producing amazing performances or songs or victories. They
feel confident because of their success, but they also feel stressed as
they try to continue that success. And here's another pressure: They
want to look a certain way while performing or playing.

Can you relate to the pressure both to achieve and to look good
while you do it? It's a lot to manage. Linking our confidence to
things our bodies can do and to how we look keeps us on a shaky
foundation, wondering where we stand with others. God offers
us a better one.

Our efforts will never be enough to satisfy us or to bring us
peace with God. We are to "glory in Christ Jesus" (Philippians

3:3) by having faith in him and dropping our frantic attempts to perform. What is of supreme worth is knowing Christ. That's why Paul could say, "I count everything as trash compared with being in Christ and knowing him." In other words, receiving Jesus's righteousness and knowing God by faith were far more precious to Paul than his past achievements or future accomplishments. He was secure and confident because he was in Christ.

When I was at my lowest moments as I struggled with my body image, God challenged my distorted thinking with today's verses. I personalized them by reminding myself that the joy of knowing Christ is better than feeling confident in my body. It's better than having the admiration of guys. It's better than feeling powerful because I'm attractive. It's better than feeling like I measure up or am in control.

For Paul, knowing Christ was the ultimate treasure—something so worthwhile that he willingly gave up everything else. Since God designed us for this, *that's* where we'll find our highest joy and greatest confidence—not in changing our bodies. I want you to live out this joy and freedom. You are free to use your gifts and abilities to point to the Lord, free to find your confidence in him, and free to shake off the pressure to "succeed" through how you look or what your body can do.

Pray: Lord Jesus, I want to join Paul in believing that knowing you is the greatest privilege in my life. Thank you for giving yourself for me and to me. Thank you for letting me know you.

Act: Read Philippians 3. What competes with Jesus for your attention and affection? What things in your life seem like better treasures than knowing Jesus?

GOD SEES THE HEART

But the LORD said to Samuel, "Do not look on his appearance or on the height of his stature, because I have rejected him. For the LORD sees not as man sees: man looks on the outward appearance, but the LORD looks on the heart." (1 Samuel 16:7)

Sadie pulled up to her new school and sat in her car, watching the students trickle in. As she got out, three guys walked by her. One elbowed his friend and laughed. "I didn't know they were letting twelve-year-olds drive now." Sadie's face burned. People constantly pointed out and even made jokes about her petite frame. Guys didn't take her seriously. Other girls ignored her in conversations, thinking she wouldn't understand what they were talking about, as if Sadie didn't have crushes or cramps or trouble with her English homework. And other people just assumed she was incompetent, like she was too young to babysit or have a job or, apparently, even drive. She hated being judged and underestimated because of her size.

In our verse today, the Lord speaks to a prophet in the Old Testament named Samuel. Samuel's job was to find the man whom God had chosen to be the next king of Israel. God sent Samuel to a certain family, and when the prophet saw a tall, handsome man among the brothers, he was impressed. Evaluating by appearance alone, Samuel assumed God had chosen that man to be king. He was wrong.

We're all like Samuel—making snap judgments based on what our eyes see. We tend to think that certain physical qualities lead to happiness or success or are a mark of God's blessing. But God isn't like us. The invisible God sees our hearts. He sees the whole picture of who we are. He sees what we worship, what we love, what we fear, and what we treasure. Although our bodies are good and important, what is in our hearts matters most to him.

Even when other people overlook us because our bodies don't fit their expectations, God's purposes for us aren't hindered. Samuel would have picked David's oldest brother to be king. But God reminded Samuel that he wanted a king who showed something more than physical attractiveness. God wanted the next king to have a heart for him. Yes, David was handsome and had beautiful eyes (1 Samuel 16:12). Yes, palace servants saw that he was a skillful musician, a brave warrior, and an eloquent and strategic leader (1 Samuel 16:18). But what mattered most? David was a "man after [God's] own heart" (1 Samuel 13:14).

Let this reading remind you that your physical appearance will not keep God from using you exactly the way he wants. God loves to surprise people with his unexpected choices (1 Corinthians 1:26–29).

Pray: God, thank you for designing my body to fulfill the purposes you have planned for me. Thank you that you see my heart and the desire you have given me to please you. I'm glad you don't judge by outward appearance like others do.

Act: Look up Psalm 57:2, Psalm 138:8, and Ephesians 1:11. What encouragement can you find in these verses for times when other people make insensitive or cruel comments?

A NEW SELF

*You have heard about [Jesus] and were taught in him, as
the truth is in Jesus, to put off your old self, which belongs to
your former manner of life and is corrupt through deceitful
desires, and to be renewed in the spirit of your minds, and
to put on the new self, created after the likeness of God in
true righteousness and holiness. (Ephesians 4:21–24)*

Jac struggled for years with obsessive thoughts about the flaws she saw in her body—how big her thighs were, how bloated her stomach felt, how puffy her face seemed. As she went through her day, she felt like she piled on weight just by breathing. Her body felt huge, as if she might not be able to fit in her car seat or through a door. Other people kept telling her how thin she looked, but she didn't believe them. She felt alone, trapped in a body she hated. She desperately needed a voice to cut through her endless negative thoughts.

Our verses today talk about how we learn to walk as new people who reflect God's holy image. As followers of Christ, we hear God's voice. His voice has the power to change our self-hating thoughts and to help us see ourselves accurately. His teaching renews our minds so that we grow in godliness.

Listening to God's voice is not a one-time event. We listen to it every day when we read the Bible. As we read, we pray and choose to believe his Word is true. His Word is living and active and discerns the thoughts and intentions of our hearts (Hebrews 4:12). Over time, it transforms the way we see ourselves. When we are tempted to follow the "deceitful desires" that corrupted us before we were saved and taught by Christ, God helps us to intentionally put off these old desires and the habits of mind and body that follow.

Jac's thoughts about her body have become debilitating as they've pushed out all other concerns. It's as if she is in a tiny room surrounded by mirrors.[1] Wherever she looks, she sees herself and hates what she sees. But she doesn't realize the mirrors are reflecting a distorted image, like a carnival's fun house mirrors.[2] Listening to God's Word will help her step out of this room of mirrors.

Every day Jac needs to take her thoughts captive (2 Corinthians 10:5). What does that mean? It means she needs to use the truths of God's Word to take charge of how she thinks. Any time she starts to think, "I'm so big. I hate the way I look," she needs to dismiss those thoughts and replace them with thoughts that represent her renewed mind.

The new thoughts might sound like "My feelings are important but not always trustworthy. I need to meditate on what *is* true instead of what *feels* true. God wants me to focus on him and how worthy and beautiful he is and how I can serve others. My size doesn't have to be the focus of my thoughts—I need to appreciate my body and look after it well. I don't need to evaluate my body beyond that. Even though it's hard for me to change my focus, God is with me, speaking truth to me through his Word."

If your struggle is similar to Jac's, there's hope for you. As you come to know God by listening to his Word and growing in holiness, you can expect your thoughts and emotions to change. Thinking rightly about your body from the Bible's perspective will slowly erode the false impressions you have of yourself. God will help you walk out of the room of mirrors and into his marvelous light.

Pray: God, please help me listen to your Word. I trust your voice more than my own perceptions. Thank you for showing me the truth and guiding me to change.

Act: When someone compliments you on your appearance, simply say "Thank you." Your mind might be screaming in protest because you don't see the beauty they see. But acknowledging their perspective will help you recalibrate your own.

NOT YOUR OWN

You are not your own, for you were bought with a price.
So glorify God in your body. (1 Corinthians 6:19–20)

JJ had convinced herself that she wasn't attractive enough for boys to notice her. After a bad haircut and months of struggling with acne, she felt worthless. So when the new guy at school started talking to her, she was surprised and thrilled. But soon she noticed that he seemed much less flirty when she wasn't wearing makeup and a cute outfit. *Whatever it takes,* she thought. *I'll do whatever it takes to keep him.* Someone else's preferences and desires had become the standard by which she made decisions about her body.

It's good for us to think about how to build others up (Romans 15:2), but pleasing them shouldn't become the all-consuming goal of our lives (Galatians 1:10), and we certainly shouldn't sin to please someone else. God's Word gives us a framework for making decisions about our bodies. In our verses today, God reminds us that we *are not our own because we have been bought with a price.* God claims us, body and soul. He loves us, and to redeem us he paid a great price—the life of his own Son. Our joyful, grateful response is to glorify God in our bodies.

When the apostle Paul wrote these verses, he was addressing a group of believers who were tempted to use their bodies sexually outside marriage. Struggles with body image sometimes lead to sexual temptation. Like JJ, we might try to prove our value by using our bodies to get guys' attention and admiration. We might develop a "whatever it takes" attitude that leads us to text inappropriate pictures of ourselves, act sexually, and more—all to prove that we are beautiful and desirable.

Knowing that we face these temptations, God has given us his rules for our good and protection. Rather than hindering our happiness, his rules free us to use our bodies in the ways he has designed us to use them—ways that lead to our flourishing. When God says, "The body is not meant for sexual immorality, but for the Lord, and the Lord for the body" (1 Corinthians 6:13), he's saving us from the devastation that comes when we use our bodies in ways that leave us confused and hurting.

We need to address the root issues that lead us to use, or consider using, our bodies to get acceptance and approval. One way for us to do this is to focus on God's love for us. Here are two passages to start you out. Psalm 90:14 is a prayer that says, "Satisfy us in the morning with your steadfast love, that we may rejoice and be glad all our days." Try asking God every morning to satisfy you with *his* love. The result of his love is joy. The second passage is Psalm 118. This psalm reminds us that we need to say over and over to ourselves, "His steadfast love endures forever."[1] Even when others seem not to notice us, God can help us cherish his steadfast, enduring love.

These two passages lift our gaze from our bodies to God and his love. As good as our bodies are, and as much as we should be thankful for them, only God's love can satisfy us and free us to walk in his ways.

Pray: Father, thank you for your steadfast, forever love. Please satisfy me with your love.

Reflect: Have you ever used your body in sexual ways to get affirmation or acceptance? Are others pressuring you to do things that you know are wrong? Talk to a mentor about any struggles that you experience in this area.

OUR NEW CITIZENSHIP

But our citizenship is in heaven, and from it we await a Savior, the Lord Jesus Christ, who will transform our lowly body to be like his glorious body, by the power that enables him even to subject all things to himself. (Philippians 3:20–21)

Different cultures have very different standards of beauty. Some cultures praise a long neck or a gap between your front teeth or a full figure. Other cultures focus on the shape of your nose or eyes or the quality and color of your skin or hair. Ideas of beauty shift from culture to culture—and even within the same culture what is "beautiful" seems to constantly change. What I perceive as attractive differs from the perception of someone who grew up in a different location or in a different time. Our definitions of beauty are fickle.

In this world, we will be pressured to meet certain beauty standards—no matter what culture we come from. But we are also citizens of a heavenly kingdom. When we become followers of the Lord Jesus, he gives us new privileges, rights, and protections. One of those privileges is a new body.

Although the apostle Paul calls our current bodies "lowly," he tells us that one day they will be transformed. When Christ returns, he will give us *new* physical bodies. They will be as different from our current bodies as flowers and trees are different from the seeds they spring from (1 Corinthians 15:37). We can't even imagine how glorious and strong our new bodies will be (1 Corinthians 15:43). We desperately need to remember this promise when our culture loudly demands that we change our bodies now to conform to its values and beauty standards.

As citizens of a heavenly kingdom, we must refuse to make our bodies into our gods. Our glorious God is stirring us up to cultivate spiritual beauty while we wait on his return. So I don't set my hope on having a healthy, attractive body now. I'm learning to set my hope fully on the grace that will be shown to me when Jesus returns (1 Peter 1:13). God will transform me when I enter his eternal kingdom, and he will take my imperfect body and give me a new, pain-free, transformed body.

As citizens of a heavenly kingdom, we will one day be united with God's people from all cultures and times. The incredible diversity of beauty that God has created will bring us joy. There won't be a sense of competition or envy. Everyone will be focused on Jesus and enjoying how their new bodies reflect his loveliness. Like a field with hundreds of types of wildflowers instead of just one, our differences will enhance the way we bring glory to God (Revelation 7:9–10).

While you resist the world's pressure to find fulfillment in your body, you should remind yourself of God's promise that your Savior will return and transform your body. You'll join the citizens of heaven as together we reflect the beauty of Jesus.

Pray: Heavenly Father, I'm so glad I'm a citizen of your kingdom. Thank you for making me your daughter and for giving me the strength to resist the pressures of the world.

Reflect: Read Matthew 5:2–16 for descriptions of what our King values. His values become our priorities as we wait for his kingdom to come. Choose one and pray for God to help you make it a bigger priority this week.

Day 24

WHEN EATING FEELS STRESSFUL

Everything created by God is good, and nothing is to be rejected if it is received with thanksgiving, for it is made holy by the word of God and prayer. (1 Timothy 4:4–5)

In college, I got the opportunity to study abroad in Costa Rica. Although my host mother was kind, she became frustrated by how much I ate, because every meal I consumed meant less money in her bank account. But I wasn't thinking about that when she told me, "You eat more than any student I've ever had." I instantly heard "you eat more" as "you are fat" and started crying. My host mom wasn't trying to shame me, but her words jabbed a painful area.

I've been ashamed of how much I eat for as long as I can remember. It took time for me to realize that even though I eat more than most women (and some men), I'm not by definition greedy or gluttonous. When I don't eat enough, I'm fatigued and prone to headaches. I need to eat! But even though I don't feel well when my body is undernourished, I've sometimes rejected the food my body needs because I've connected eating with gaining weight. God intended for food to be a nourishing gift for us to enjoy, but it became something I agonized over.

Do you dread making decisions about food? When we are struggling with our body image, eating can feel like a burden rather than a good gift. The difficulty involved in making food decisions is compounded by a diet culture that constantly tells us what we should—or shouldn't—be eating. Also, we may realize that we use food as an escape or a refuge. Eating will certainly be stressful if we use food to help ourselves deal with difficult relationships or troubling situations. It might feel easier to avoid food so we don't have to wrestle with how our hearts are doing or how we can honor God with what we eat. But God wants our meals to be times of joy and thanksgiving, not stress.

People haven't changed much in the two thousand years since the New Testament was written. Some teachers complicated God's gift of food by teaching that it was most spiritual to reject the pleasure of eating. They "require[d] abstinence from foods that God created to be received with thanksgiving by those who believe and know the truth" (1 Timothy 4:3).

But true spirituality includes being mindful of God and dependent on the Holy Spirit *while we enjoy his gifts*. Food is a gift because it gives us opportunities to direct our hearts to God, remembering that he generously provides for us. We can respond with gratitude for the nourishment of food and the pleasure of eating. Food is also a gift because it gives us opportunities to bless others. We do that whenever we share a meal, whenever we are generous with the food we have, and whenever we consider other people's dietary needs and culinary preferences as more important than our own. God wants us to eat in faith, tasting his goodness and generosity and extending it to others.

Pray: God, thank you for providing food to nourish me. Help me to notice the temperatures, textures, flavors, and colors of my food and to savor your goodness in giving me such variety. Help me crave you as much as I crave my favorite food.

Act: If you have habits of binging or purging, please speak with someone who can help. Look for people in your family or your church who can encourage you to move toward the Lord and experience freedom from these habits. You don't have to stay stuck in a confused relationship with food.

RESTORED TO GOD

And I heard a loud voice from the throne saying, "Behold, the dwelling place of God is with man. He will dwell with them, and they will be his people, and God himself will be with them as their God." (Revelation 21:3)

God delights to be with his people and to be their greatest joy and treasure. Because nothing can take him away from us, we can't lose our source of joy. As God purifies our hearts so that we can enjoy him more and more, our perspective on our bodies changes. We think differently because we see life through the lens of God's character.

God has done everything necessary to restore us to a right relationship with himself. But even though we have been restored to God and find satisfaction in him, that doesn't mean that our struggles are over. The Bible is honest about this: Even though our bodies are good gifts for us to steward and use in ways that point people to our great Savior, life in our earthly bodies is difficult. We groan because our bodies are not yet what they will be (Romans 8:23). We groan, but we groan with hope. One day when Jesus comes again, we will have perfect, resurrected bodies (1 Corinthians 15:40–49; Philippians 3:21). As we anticipate that day, we cling to his promises and follow his voice.

One day, when you are restored to God in the fullest sense, you will not be troubled by your body. No sin or shame will taint your perspective. Your body will function perfectly, and you will be delighted by how it reflects the glory of God. You will be gloriously free to enjoy God and the new world he has created.

DO YOU KNOW HOW TO FEAR THE LORD?

*Charm is deceitful, and beauty is vain, but a woman
who fears the LORD is to be praised. (Proverbs 31:30)*

I recently watched an interview with a former successful model who is now in her fifties. With tears streaming down her face, she said she no longer felt valued. Because her face and body had changed, she didn't feel seen or heard. She didn't know who she was. My heart broke for her. This woman hadn't planned to base her life on her appearance. It was her job as a model to look attractive, stay fit, and wear gorgeous clothes. But in the end she had built her life on a foundation that was fleeting. A woman who fears the Lord knows that the foundation for her life is based not on her appearance but on God's love for her and her obedience to him.

I want to introduce you to another beautiful woman. Her name was Abigail, and she was married to a rich man named Nabal. The Bible says Nabal was "harsh and badly behaved" (1 Samuel 25:3). His foolishness brought his whole household into danger.

At that time in Israel, King Saul was trying to kill God's chosen king, David. As David and his men roamed the countryside, avoiding assassins sent by Saul, they protected Nabal's shepherds and animals, the source of Nabal's wealth. David could have enriched himself at Nabal's expense, but instead he looked after Nabal and his interests. Yet even though David had provided a valuable service, Nabal refused to acknowledge his kindness or offer even the most basic gestures of hospitality: when David and his men were hungry, Nabal withheld the food that he could easily have given them. His rudeness infuriated David, and David decided to retaliate by killing all the men in Nabal's household.

When Abigail learned of David's plans, she loaded donkeys with food and drink and went to meet his oncoming warriors. Her gifts and her words of wisdom turned away David's anger and saved many lives. After she gently reminded David that God was working on his behalf (1 Samuel 25:23–31), David praised her. In front of his warriors and Abigail's servants, David told her that she was blessed. Her fear of the Lord amazed him.

When we talk about Abigail's fear of the Lord, we mean she was humbly delighted to know and obey God. She focused on God and considered how he would want her to act, even if it meant sacrificing her time, money, and comfort—and even taking a dangerous risk. She loved and admired God so much that she had compassion on her foolish husband and her angry king. Soon after, God brought judgment on her husband, and he died. When David heard about Nabal's death, he asked Abigail to be his wife. She became part of Israel's royal family and is remembered and praised as a woman who feared the Lord.

The fear of the Lord guides us, establishes our values, changes what we want, and gives us new hopes and goals. It's the right foundation for our lives. No matter how our appearance might change, we can be steady and hopeful because the source of our life is God, not how we look.

Pray: God, thank you for giving me a foundation for my life that doesn't shift based on how I look. Please help me find my deepest delight in knowing you.

Reflect: The term *fear of the Lord* can be confusing. How does Abigail's life help you understand what it means to fear the Lord?

BEAUTY THAT IS PRECIOUS TO GOD

Do not let your adorning be external—the braiding of hair and the putting on of gold jewelry, or the clothing you wear—but let your adorning be the hidden person of the heart with the imperishable beauty of a gentle and quiet spirit, which in God's sight is very precious. (1 Peter 3:3–4)

Sometimes when I go to the gym for a spin class, I see a woman who looks ready for the runway. Cute hair, jewelry, mascara, even some lipstick. She looks nice. But she's gone to a lot of effort to produce a look that sweat will trickle away in ten minutes. It makes me wonder if she's in the class for a different reason than the rest of us.

Our decisions about how we adorn ourselves send a message. We communicate something about ourselves and our purpose by what we wear.

The apostle Peter talks about our life purpose in a fascinating way. He says God has chosen us, given us mercy, and loved us as his own so that we "may proclaim the excellencies of him who called you out of darkness into his marvelous light" (1 Peter 2:9). That's one way to understand the point of our lives. The rest of Peter's first letter talks about what it looks like for us to proclaim God's excellencies in our relationships and in our suffering. That brings us to our verses for today. Peter tells us that we can communicate what God values—what he sees as precious—by how we adorn ourselves.

Peter wants you to focus on cultivating a beauty that can't be messed up by sweat or wind or rain or a bad hair day. A beauty that can't be taken off by a thief or a washcloth. A beauty that isn't affected by sickness or disability. God reminds us to value, and focus on cultivating, a beauty that's hidden but so powerful that it doesn't fade. This inner beauty is very precious to God.

Peter isn't telling women to stop caring about how they look or dress. But he doesn't want us to concentrate on the external, which is perishable. He is calling us to turn our focus to the imperishable beauty of a heart that honors God and submits to him.

Peter goes on to explain what this beauty looks like. It is gentle and quiet. This means that we are not defined by anger or fear. We are gentle with others because we aren't competing for anyone's attention or affection. We are steady because we know that God loves us and will help us appreciate and use our bodies in ways that honor him. We graciously accept God's decisions for our lives—even the ones that affect our bodies—knowing that he is working all things for our good. This perspective brings us peace and fills our spirits with a lovely quietness.

God is calling you to grow in an imperishable beauty. You might do this in all kinds of ways. Instead of coloring your hair, you could donate to someone in need. Instead of buying new jewelry, you could save to go on a mission trip. Instead of planning a new diet, you could serve meals at a homeless shelter. Instead of stressing about what to wear to an event, you could plan to talk to someone who is shy. The joy of serving others helps us shift our focus to things that last forever.

God has given you everything you need to grow in godly beauty (2 Peter 1:3). Physical adornments will wear out, fall apart, get lost, and cease to fit. The adornment that changes your heart will last forever.

Pray: God, thank you for telling me what is precious to you and helping me grow in the beauty of a gentle and quiet spirit.

Act: Trusting God is the foundation of a gentle and quiet heart. Read the following verses and journal about how they help you trust God: Psalm 147:5; Isaiah 46:9–10; 54:10; Romans 8:18–39.

TRAIN FOR GODLINESS

Train yourself for godliness; for while bodily training is of some value, godliness is of value in every way, as it holds promise for the present life and also for the life to come. (1 Timothy 4:7–8)

In my late teens, I came across a study that suggested that intense exercise is as effective as antidepressants for alleviating depression. I latched on to that thought. I felt better when I exercised. But using exercise as my main way to tackle stress helped me justify my exercise habits to people who questioned whether I was working out too much or too intensely.

The apostle Paul gives us the wisdom we need to enjoy the gift of exercise and use it to our advantage without missing our bigger need: to grow in godliness—which means to become more like the Lord Jesus. Although exercise has value now, godliness has even more value because it promises good things for this life *and* the one to come.

Let's start with the simple truth that physical exercise is genuinely worthwhile. God made our bodies to move, so physical movement is a gift that increases our health and our joy. Regular exercise helps our bodies feel and work better. Getting outside, walking, swimming, and riding a bike are ways to relieve stress while also strengthening our muscles and bones.

We overlook these benefits if we focus on exercise solely as a way to improve our physical appearance. We can use physical strength and fitness to love and serve God and others—or we can use it as a way to serve ourselves. We might exercise intensely, trying to perfect our bodies. We might avoid exercise to sidestep the discomfort of exertion and a growing sense of failure when we don't meet the body standards of the gym crowd. Fitness has so many definitions that we may get overwhelmed and stop trying to make progress. We may think, "What's the use? I'll never look the way I want, so why bother?" This attitude misses the point. Training our bodies has value because it strengthens us to better serve others and fulfill our God-given roles. Exercise is part of the privilege of stewarding our bodies.

But it's crucial that we don't make this aspect of our stewardship all-important. This is why Paul contrasts bodily training with godliness. When we worship God and obey him, our character changes to become more like our Savior's.

What does bodily training look like when it's done in a godly way? It means that we don't become irritable when circumstances interfere with our plans to exercise or eat a certain way. It means that we thank God for our bodies and pray for others when we exercise instead of focusing on how many calories we're burning. It means that we choose to be content with what our bodies look like when we are eating and exercising in moderation. It means that we are kind to others who aren't physically able to do what we can. It means that we wait on those who are weaker or slower than us and help them instead of grumbling or bragging. It means that we persist in stewarding our bodies even when our appearance doesn't change or doesn't change as quickly as we want. Ultimately, godliness means that we use our bodies to help others, even if we are fearful of being shamed because of how we look. We don't let fears about our bodies stop us from doing good.

Pray: God, please help me steward my body well. Help me see both the value of bodily training and the supreme value of godliness.

Reflect: Do you gravitate toward too much exercise or too little? What motivates you to exercise?

FOOD DECISIONS

"All things are lawful for me," but not all things are helpful. "All things are lawful for me," but I will not be dominated by anything. "Food is meant for the stomach and the stomach for food." (1 Corinthians 6:12–13)

Cheese curls or green beans? Cupcakes or steak? Candy or blueberries? Are some of these choices more godly than the others? The answer from God's Word might surprise you.

The Christians in ancient Corinth had the slogan "All things are lawful for me" (or "I have the right to do anything"—NIV). They liked to trot out that saying whenever they wanted to rationalize indulging in a bodily pleasure without having to think about God and his ways. When they applied their motto to food, it might have sounded like this: "I have a stomach. It was designed to enjoy food. So I can shovel in all the food I want. That's why my stomach exists." They didn't believe they should deny their bodies any pleasure they were capable of experiencing. But God corrected their mistaken thinking through the writing of the apostle Paul. We have bodies that can enjoy so many things. That's a wonderful gift from God. But we must also consider which of those pleasures are helpful to us and which have the potential to dominate or enslave us.

Food does not bring us near to God (1 Corinthians 8:8). We have to make choices about food based on what is *wise* for us to eat, not because we think that certain foods are themselves morally good or bad. We can enjoy cheese curls and candy in a way that honors God. He really did design our bodies to experience a delightful variety of flavors and textures. In his kindness, he allows us to make decisions related to food for both our enjoyment and our physical health.

When we're deciding what to eat, the most important question isn't "Is this food bad?" Instead, we need to ask other questions.

The first question might be "Is this food helpful?" There are several ways we can answer. We may realize that certain foods help us to be more alert, to have more energy, or to sleep better. We may come to see that the way we eat either helps us be ready to love and serve others or makes us grumpy, tired, bloated, or even sick. I started making a connection between my mood and my sugar intake when I was a teenager. I began to realize if I ate sugar too much or too often, I didn't feel well. Sugar isn't bad. It just wasn't helpful to me when I made it a regular part of my day. Even when I knew that, it was still hard to say no.

That's why Paul suggests in these verses a second question that we can ask ourselves: "Does this food dominate me? Do I obey it like it's my master?" It may be that a particular food has grown into a demanding monster. Here are some follow-up questions you can ask yourself: *Can I eat this in moderation? Do I avoid food that other people have prepared for me so I can indulge in this instead? Do I avoid others while eating this? Do I daydream about this food when I'm stressed or lonely or tired? Do I forget to thank God for this food?*

Paul wants us to know that the body's ultimate purpose is not to derive pleasure from a created thing. Our bodies are meant for the Lord (1 Corinthians 6:13). The pleasure we get from food is a good gift for us to enjoy, but it's not our only consideration. We also need to think about what's helpful to us and what might dominate us. God alone is to be our master. And he's the best master there is.

Pray: Lord, please show me how to eat wisely in a spirit of freedom. Thank you for the guidance you give me in your Word.

Reflect: Do you feel guilty when you enjoy certain foods? Do you imagine that you would be a better person or more acceptable to God if you avoided certain foods? What are those foods? Why do you think some foods are hard for you to eat in moderation?

GUARDING YOUR HEART AND TREASURING YOUR GOD

Above all else, guard your heart, for everything
you do flows from it. (Proverbs 4:23 NIV)

Do your body-image struggles seem worse when you are scrolling social media on your phone? We often don't think about guarding our hearts when we use our phones. But our verse today tells us to guard our hearts "above all else." Guarding our hearts means watching what we worship so that nothing else can slip in to take priority over God.[1] It means noticing what captures our hearts' attention and admiration. One of the ways we walk in the wisdom of this verse has to do with how we use our phones.

Social media images "get inside us, shape us, and form our lives in ways that compete with God's design for our focus and worship."[2] Although social media helps us make connections, it also tracks our interests and gives us more and more content to feed our obsessions. It cultivates our appetites and trains us to value and pursue certain things. It silently gives us a value system that we need to analyze in the light of God's Word.[3]

There are lots of ways for us to guard our hearts. Here are three.

First, you can guard your heart by committing to reading, hearing, or meditating on God's Word before you get on social media each day. When your first moments and thoughts each day are centered on God, you are focusing your worship on your Savior and fixing your attention on his beauty. This can help you remember that no matter how amazing your body is (or isn't) and no matter how many people applaud you online or in person (or don't), no created thing is able to fill the void in your heart. You are designed to treasure Christ and be filled by him. When you treasure anything else, you'll be left empty and confused.

Second, think about what drives you to your phone. Do you use it to connect with friends? Are you bored? Are you drawn by the thrill you get from likes and views? You may be able to understand your motives better if you slow down as you interact with social media. The faster you scroll, the stronger your appetite becomes for the next burst of novelty—and the less time you have for reflection. Since social media has the power to deepen your appetites for worldly things, you need to be on guard.

As you slow down, here are some questions to consider: *Does looking at this account fuel my preoccupation with my body? Do I feel like I have to buy something or change how I look to keep up with current beauty trends? Do I compare myself with the people I see? What feelings do I have after spending fifteen minutes on social media? Does time on my phone help me treasure God or encourage me to ignore him? Am I able to go for several days without social media?*

Finally, it's a good idea to make a plan before you start scrolling and decide how much time you will spend online. Reducing the amount of time you are staring into a screen won't change your heart, but it will create space for you to connect to God and those who are physically around you.

Guarding your heart is really important. As you take these steps, remember your ultimate goal. Your heart is meant to be filled with Christ, not the things of the world—one satisfies, while the other will only leave you longing for more.

Pray: God, please help me understand how important it is for me to guard my heart. Forgive me when I'm more interested in the things of the world than in you.

Act: Commit with a friend to reading the Bible before you get on your phone each morning. Try reading the gospel of John, one chapter each day for a month. Share something from that chapter with your friend.

WISDOM FOR HARD PLACES

Set your minds on things that are above, not on things that are on earth. (Colossians 3:2)

Some places and situations bring pressures that are unique or intense. It might be a wedding or a party or the first day of school. Maybe it's a relative's house where you are under watchful eyes and constant critique. Maybe it's the pool or the beach or the lake, where everyone is in bathing suits. We don't need to be afraid of these places, but we do need to prepare for them. I wonder which places are hard for you.

We need to make wise plans before we face these situations. Colossians 3:2 reminds us of a command God has given to help us: We are to intentionally focus our thoughts on things that are above, where Christ is. The next verse tells us why. We have died, and our lives are hidden with Christ. The most important thing that's true about us—that we belong to Jesus and are his servants—is not outwardly visible. Since our lives are with Christ, we do well to joyfully make the effort to think about him more and more.

To set our minds on things above, we need to understand what "things on earth" are. God isn't telling us to refuse to think about people or to avoid the good things he has made. The next few verses explain that "things on earth" are things like sexual immorality, impurity, evil passions and desires, covetousness, and idolatry (Colossians 3:5–10). Paul wants us to center our lives on Christ and to fix our hearts on his ways by putting these earthly sins to death rather than indulging in them. Fighting these earthly behaviors starts with thinking about how Jesus wants us to serve and love others.

So when you're somewhere where you feel more shame than usual about your body or are tempted to compare yourself to other people (whether they're in formal dresses or bathing suits), God equips you to have a heavenly mindset.

The next time you're struggling, remind yourself, "The people around me are more than just bodies. They're individuals with stories and personalities and problems." You can pray that the people you see would come to know Jesus as their Savior. Remind yourself, "A beautiful body doesn't equal an easy or fun life. Even beautiful people suffer." Focus on the beauty of nature. If you're outside, you can enjoy God's gifts of warm sunshine, cool water, colorful sunsets, or majestic mountains. Try thanking God for opportunities to focus on him and on people you love, and ask him to give you an opportunity to encourage someone. Or ask, "Where can I find ways to serve?" Maybe you'll see an elderly person you could chat with or a child you could play with. Maybe someone needs help serving food or moving tables or collecting trash. There are always opportunities to help others. Your body is useful. Thinking this way will help you get your focus off yourself and what your body looks like.

Pray: Heavenly Father, thank you for helping me set my mind on you. Please help me cultivate a heart of gratitude that gives you thanks in every situation because you are with me.[1]

Act: Find one way to serve someone else this week. It might be at a special event, or it might simply be in your home with your family. Commit to finding a way to lighten someone's burden and encourage them.

Day 31

JOYFUL TRANSFORMATION

We all, with unveiled face, beholding the glory of the Lord, are being transformed into the same image from one degree of glory to another. (2 Corinthians 3:18)

If God had a physical body, what would you expect him to look like? Amazingly, some people in the first century got the chance to find out. When God the Son came to earth as the Jesus of history, he wasn't physically impressive (Isaiah 53:2), he nonetheless showed us how to steward and appreciate our bodies and use them for God's purposes. By taking on flesh and blood, he forever crushed the idea that our bodies are somehow bad or gross. He died a physical, bodily death in our place. Then he rose from the dead—still in a physical body—to show that he had won victory over death and to assure us that one day he will give us perfect, redeemed bodies like his (Philippians 3:21).

Although we can no longer see our Savior with physical eyes, he has given us spiritual sight so we can perceive his beauty. When we repent and put our faith in the Lord, God lifts the veil that kept us from seeing the glory of Jesus our Savior. We are transformed as we behold Jesus—transformed so that we better reflect the divine beauty of the Son of God. This transformation means that we will love Jesus more and more—and reflect him more and more in how we live. Out of our love for him, we can rejoice that our bodies are able to fulfill his purposes, no matter what they look like.

This joy is possible because we are gazing at Jesus. "In the Lord Jesus, God has given us someone who is absolute beauty, truth, and goodness all the way through . . . no dark side, no secret vices, no selfishness that comes out now and then. He only speaks truth; he only loves what is right; he never serves himself."[1] This is supreme beauty. As we grow closer to Jesus and this beauty washes over us, we will experience increasing joy over how God has ordered our lives.

We can enjoy putting the spotlight on Jesus rather than on our physical appearance (Psalm 115:1). We can be joyful that God has created our bodies to do good works (Ephesians 2:10). We can be excited to use our bodies to proclaim the excellencies of Jesus Christ, who called us out of darkness into his marvelous light (1 Peter 2:9). We can joyfully honor God with our bodies by loving and serving others (Philippians 2:3–4). We can be content because, when we know Christ, we have true riches and eternal life; we know that someday our bodies will be made gloriously perfect (Mark 8:35–36; John 17:3).

We get to spend our lives and our eternity with our stunningly beautiful Savior. As we look forward to eternity, we can thank God for his wisdom in giving us the bodies, and the lives, that we have.

Pray: God, thank you for saving me and giving me joy while you change me. Help me to keep my eyes locked on Jesus and to adore him more and more.

Reflect: Read Isaiah 52:13–53:12. Isaiah tells us that Jesus was wounded and killed so we can be forgiven and have peace with God. Thank God for Jesus and his sacrifice for you.

CONCLUSION

I bounced from foot to foot, trying to shake off the pre-race jitters. The other competitors paced around, ready to begin the triathlon. I shivered in the chilly air as I thought about diving into the waves. When the gun went off, we raced into the water, and, as I jumped into the surf, I tried to memorize the position of the guide buoy.

One of the hardest things about swimming in the ocean is the feeling that you aren't making any progress. You're working hard, but you can't tell whether you've moved an inch. The waves disorient you. Other swimmers kick or elbow you as they navigate the swells. You suddenly think about the possibility of sharks. Your goggles fill with salt water. You are kicking and moving your arms, but you can't sense any momentum.

Body-image struggles can sometimes feel like this. Maybe you are working to fill your heart with truth. You are renewing your mind with Scripture. You are clinging to God's promises. You are fighting to treasure Christ. But it seems like you are stuck. This part of the struggle might catch you off guard. The key is to remember that, as you hold on to Christ, Christ is holding on to you. By his Spirit's work in your life, you *are* making progress. You are moving forward and getting closer to the finish line. When I was in the ocean and the murky water and the waves disoriented me, I didn't need a new strategy. I just needed to keep doing what I was doing: breathing, taking the next stroke, kicking my legs.

We can get disoriented and disheartened as we run the race of faith. We need to be reminded of truths that help us settle in and run with endurance. That's what God gives us in Hebrews 12:1–2: "Therefore, since we are surrounded by so great a cloud of witnesses, let us also lay aside every weight, and sin which clings so closely, and let us run with endurance the race that is set before us, looking to Jesus, the founder and perfecter of our faith, who for the joy that was set before him endured the cross, despising the shame, and is seated at the right hand of the throne of God."

These verses are loaded with encouragements to help us in our race. Their central point is that we need to run with endurance *while looking to Jesus.* What do we see when we look to Jesus? We see the founder and perfecter of our faith. He *gives* us our faith, and he *completes* it. We also see that he endured by concentrating on the joy his Father had promised him. Through Jesus's example, God reminds us of the joy that comes from running for him and the joy we will experience at the finish line.

Although Jesus had to run the hardest part of his race alone, we don't. Our heavenly Father never leaves us. He is *with* us. Even more than a coach who jogs the last mile with you, Jesus puts life and energy into our bodies and souls to get us to the finish line. He encourages us and helps us at every step. He never leaves us, and he equips us with everything we need so that we can do his will (Hebrews 13:5, 21).

Not only do we have Jesus's presence, we also have the joy of running with others. When I did my first triathlon, the camaraderie of the race surprised me. Strangers cheered for me. Racers changed flat bicycle tires for others, shared water and snacks, and waited for friends who got tangled up in the transition area. It's easy to see others as competition, but we are all created in the image of God. And if those around us are believers, we are all on one team, part of the same family, members of the same body (1 Corinthians 12:12). It's part of our mission and our joy to help others make it to the finish line—and to benefit from their help and encouragement.

Hebrews 12:1 also says that we are surrounded by a cloud of witnesses. We have an audience for our spiritual race. From the pages of the Bible, other believers shout reminders about how faithful God is—they tell us we can make it when we rely on him. Their testimony of overcoming obstacles encourages us and keeps us focused on what matters most.

Although I wasn't surrounded by a cloud of people, I had an audience for my triathlon too. Usually an audience makes us focus a lot more on how we look. But during the race I wasn't thinking about that. I hadn't taken a makeup bag or picked out fashionable clothes. Too many other things occupied my mind. I focused on the next mile, my teammates, and the obstacles on the course. By the end, I was salty, sweaty, muddy, and bloody from a tumble. But I made it. My friends made it too. That's what counted—and that was where the joy came from.

Christ has made us his own. We don't run to earn his favor. We run because he has set his affection on us and has chosen us to be his. When we are justified by Jesus, we begin our race of faith. We cross the finish line when we close our eyes in death and open them in eternity with our Savior. We'll have new, glorified bodies and be totally free from sin and suffering. We will have complete joy as we live with Jesus and worship him forever.

ACKNOWLEDGMENTS

"Not that we are sufficient in ourselves to claim anything as coming from us, but our sufficiency is from God" (2 Corinthians 3:5). This book is in your hands because God uses weak strugglers and patiently works in us and through us for his glory. Knowing Christ and speaking about him are the highest joys and privileges in life. I thank God for his grace and patience. I also thank him for sending kind, wise people to encourage, help, and challenge me.

First, a thank-you to my husband, Darien. Thank you for expanding my vision of what God might do in my life. Thank you for your patience and consistent encouragement. Thank you for helping me keep going.

Dad and Mom, thank you for your faithful example of Christ-likeness. Thank you for your prayers and encouragement and never-failing love for your family. I'm thrilled that we can talk about biblical counseling together.

Amy Baker, thank you for your patient, gentle counsel. You help me see the Lord Jesus more clearly and treasure him more deeply.

Andee Ellerbee, thank you for faithful friendship and care. Your wisdom and help have been invaluable.

Jenny Solomon, thank you for being a dear friend—a friend who kept gently nudging me to write, helping me when I got stuck, and tenderly caring for me.

Curtis Solomon, thank you for giving me my first opportunity to blog at the Biblical Counseling Coalition and for continuing to open doors so I could grow as a counselor and as a writer.

Chelsea Erickson, thank you for your enthusiasm and encouragement. Your kind words helped me see that I might have something to share from God's Word about body image.

To all the people who prayed and cared for me through this process, thank you for cheering me on and being an essential part of God's work in my life. I'm grateful.

NOTES

DAY 2: CREATED IN GOD'S IMAGE

1. See Philip Ryken, *Beauty Is Your Destiny: How the Promise of Splendor Changes Everything* (Crossway, 2023).

DAY 4: CRAFTED WITH CARE

1. Emma Scrivener, "Don't Take Yourself for Granted," *A New Name* (blog), May 21, 2014, https://www.emmascrivener.net/2014/05/dont-take-yourself-for-granted/.
2. Carol Torgan, "Humans Can Identify More Than 1 Trillion Smells," National Institutes of Health, March 31, 2014, https://www.nih.gov/news-events/nih-research-matters/humans-can-identify-more-1-trillion-smells.
3. Mary Alexander, "Yes, Our Stomach Acid Can Theoretically Dissolve Some Metals—But Don't Try It at Home," Africa Check, September 8, 2022, https://africacheck.org/fact-checks/meta-programme-fact-checks/yes-our-stomach-acid-can-theoretically-dissolve-some-metals.
4. Russel Lazarus, "How Does the Eye Work?" Optometrists Network, accessed January 29, 2025, https://www.optometrists.org/general-practice-optometry/guide-to-eye-health/how-does-the-eye-work/.

DAY 5: EXPERIENCING GOD'S GOODNESS

1. John Piper, "I'm Obsessed with My Appearance—How Can I Stop?" Desiring God, October 19, 2020, https://www.desiringgod.org/interviews/im-obsessed-with-my-appearance-how-can-i-stop.

DAY 6: GOD'S GIFT OF GENDER

1. For more, see Rebecca McLaughlin, *Jesus Through the Eyes of Women: How the First Female Disciples Help Us Know and Love the Lord* (The Gospel Coalition, 2022) and Abigail Dodds, *A Student's Guide to Womanhood* (Christian Focus Publications, 2022).

DAY 10: EXPOSED TO SHAME

1. For help with shame, see Edward T. Welch, *Shame Interrupted: How God Lifts the Pain of Worthlessness and Rejection* (New Growth Press, 2012).

DAY 14: DESPERATE FOR CONTROL

1. Edward T. Welch, *Eating Disorders: The Quest for Thinness* (New Growth Press, 2008), 10.

DAY 15: ENVY KILLS JOY

1. Tilly Dillehay, *Seeing Green* (Harvest House, 2018), 39–40.

DAY 18: YOU ARE A STEWARD

1. See Zach Schlegel, "Refuge in the God Who Is Sovereign," April 12, 2015, Capitol Hill Baptist Church, Washington, DC, audio recording, 57:00, https://www.capitolhillbaptist.org/sermon/refuge-in-the-god-who-is-sovereign/.
2. Schlegel.

DAY 21: A NEW SELF

1. See John Piper, "My Body: Friend or Foe?" Desiring God, May 7, 2018, https://www.desiringgod.org/interviews/my-body-friend-or-foe.
2. See Julie Lowe, "I Struggle with Body Image Issues. What Do I Do?" Christian Counseling & Educational Foundation,

July 23, 2016, video, 4:03, https://www.ccef.org/video/broken
-body-image-0.

DAY 22: NOT YOUR OWN

1. Amy Baker, *Why Do I Care? When Others' Approval Matters
Too Much* (New Growth Press, 2016), 9.

DAY 29: GUARDING YOUR HEART AND TREASURING YOUR GOD

1. Sean Perron and Spencer Harmon, *Letters to a Romantic: On
Dating* (P&R Publishing, 2017), 92.
2. Tony Reinke, *Competing Spectacles: Treasuring Christ in the
Media Age* (Crossway, 2019), 118.
3. Tony Reinke, "How Do I Resist Smartphone Overuse?"
Desiring God, March 8, 2019, https://www.desiringgod.org
/interviews/how-do-i-resist-smartphone-overuse.
1. See Amy Baker, "Controlling Our Thinking," 2023, NorthCreek
Church, Walnut Creek, California, 58:30, https://nctconfer
ence.org/workshop-audio#/message/amy-baker-controlling
-our-thinking-women-only-478.

DAY 31: JOYFUL TRANSFORMATION

1. David Gibson, *Radically Whole: Gospel Healing for the Divided
Heart* (Crossway, 2022), 88.

RECOMMENDED RESOURCES

Baker, Amy. *Managing Your Emotions: Keeping Your Feelings from Running the Show*. New Growth Press, 2013. [Big emotions accompany struggles with body image. This booklet gives a biblical overview of feelings, how they become disordered, and how to appreciate and use them in the way God designed.]

Emlet, Michael R. *Overeating: When Enough Isn't Enough*. New Growth Press, 2019. [This booklet helps readers consider reasons they might overeat and what the Bible says about food. It also gives practical advice for eating.]

Fitzpatrick, Elyse. *Love to Eat, Hate to Eat: Breaking the Bondage of Destructive Eating Habits*. Harvest House, 2020. [This book explores the reasons eating habits become harmful and shows how to change.]

McLaughlin, Rebecca. *Jesus Through the Eyes of Women: How the First Female Disciples Help Us Know and Love the Lord*. The Gospel Coalition, 2022. [Seeing Jesus's interactions with and care for his female disciples helps us appreciate the role we've been given as women to reflect the beauty of our Savior.]

Ryken, Philip. *Beauty Is Your Destiny: How the Promise of Splendor Changes Everything*. Crossway, 2023. [This book describes how God defines beauty and the value he places on making his people beautiful.]

Schlegel, Zach. *Fearing Others: Putting God First*. P&R Publishing, 2019. [This 31-day devotional equips readers to recognize people-pleasing in their lives and gives them the wisdom and tools to make changes.]

Welch, Edward T. *Eating Disorders: The Quest for Thinness*. New Growth Press, 2008. [Eating disorders can be part of body-image struggles. This booklet gives an overview of the heart issues involved in eating disorders and offers practical strategies that lead to hope and change.]

Rooted Ministry's mission is to equip and empower churches and parents to faithfully disciple students toward lifelong faith in Jesus Christ. Our vision is to transform youth and family ministry so that every student receives grace-filled, gospel-centered, and Bible-saturated discipleship in the church and at home.

Rooted was born in response to the crisis in the spiritual lives of young people. What started with a small conference has grown into a movement to see gospel-centered youth ministry become the normative experience of teenagers throughout the church. Rooted promotes gospel-centered youth ministry through books, conferences, curricula, and courses.

Rooted's 2021 release, *The Jesus I Wish I Knew in High School*, features stories from thirty authors about bullying, eating disorders, addiction, racism, family conflict, and the intense pressure to achieve, demonstrating how knowing Jesus brings rest and healing. In 2023, P&R Publishing and Rooted launched the series 31-Day Devotionals for Teenagers. The first book in the series, Liz Edrington's *Anxiety: Finding the Better Story*, won The Gospel Coalition's 2023 book award for devotional literature.

Rooted embraces a simple approach to youth ministry based on our understanding of Scripture and validated by research on effective models for cultivating sustainable faith in young people. We emphasize five pillars of youth ministry: gospel centrality, theological depth through biblical teaching, relational discipleship, partnership with parents, and integration with the whole church body.

Rooted uses this framework to promote faithful discipleship of young people through the adults who love them. Imagine the impact on teenagers' lives if each week they are taught God's Word, prayed for, and mentored to understand God's grace for them through Christ. Rooted is reaching thousands of students by equipping their leaders for this type of meaningful ministry.

To learn more about Rooted, visit www.rootedministry.com.